Kafkaland

Kafkaland

Prejudice, Law and Counterterrorism in India

Manisha Sethi

Three Essays
COLLECTIVE

First Edition October 2014

ISBN 978-93-83968-00-8

Three Essays
COLLECTIVE

Three Essays Collective, B-957 Palam Vihar,
GURGAON (Haryana) 122 017 India
Tel: 91-124 236 9023, +91 98681 26587
www.threeessays.com

Printed at Chaman Offset Printers, New Delhi

To the memory of

Saurabh 'Bittu' Sethi,
musician, brother, who left us too early

and

Mukul Sinha,
who taught us never to fear

Contents

Acknowledgements

This book is the product of the collective energies of many people. First, my colleagues and comrades at Jamia Teachers' Solidarity Association – Sanghamitra, Sohaib, Adil, Ghazi bhai, Farah, Azra, Ambarien, Bhatt Saab, Nipa, Manoj, Rahul and others – our work together is at the core of this book.

"Crime and Punishment" and "Sinful Liberals and the Investigative Bias" have been published earlier on the blog *Kafila.org* (the former as "Delhi Police Special Cell: Encounters, Frame up, Impunity"). A shorter version of the chapter on Malegaon was published in *Outlook* as "Who Traced the RDX?" (29 July 2009). A long essay commissioned by *Hardnews* is also reproduced here; an earlier version of "Terrorism's True Lies" was also published in *Hardnews*. These pieces have been revised and updated wherever necessary. I am thankful to the publishers and editors for publishing my articles and then graciously allowing me to draw upon them for use in this volume. Thanks to Shuddhabrata Sengupta, Sanjay Kapoor and Saba Naqvi for their support. The chapter on encounter killings was presented at a seminar at Nehru Memorial Museum and Library. I am thankful to colleagues at NMML for their comments. Asad Zaidi saw a book where I didn't. He was a most patient and indulgent publisher.

The generosity of many people has sustained this work.

In Delhi: Shabnam Hashmi, Vrinda Grover, Abu Zafar, Ranganath Singh, Kumar Sundaram, Mazin Khan, Dr. Zafrul Islam Khan, Iftikhar Gilani, Muzamil and Paramjeet;
In Karnataka: Akmal Razvi, Sidharth Narrain, Imran Khan, Musab Iqbal, Tariq, Irshad Desai, Muthiur Rehman and Aijaz Mirza;
In Mumbai: Yug Mohit Chaudhuri and Sharib Ali;
In Madhya Pradesh: Ansar Indori, Shafeeque Siddiqi, Imran, Sarfaraz and Noor Mohammad Advocate;
In Uttar Pradesh: Shoaib Mohhamad, Tariq Shafeeque, Masihuddin Sanjari, Rajiv Yadav, Shahnawaz and Ravindra Rai;
Gulam Rabanni *in Hyderabad*.

I am beholden to the NMML for allowing me the time and freedom to undertake the travels necessary for this work.

I am grateful for the good counsel of Trideep Pais, Jawahar Raja, Mayur Suresh, Rajat Kumar, Sarim Naved, Ashwath Sitharaman, Salar Khan and Ashok Agrwaal. Special thanks are owed to Sushant Sinha of *Indiankanoon.org* who can magically retrieve any untraceable judgement upon request; to Venkatesh Nayak, who is a wizard with RTIs, and to Subasri Krishnan for lending me her excellent film, *This or that Particular Person*. Rajeev Kumar prepared the tables on budget illustrating the comparative expenditure on defence.

My fellow travellers in this journey – Mahtab and Mansi – thank you for the comradeship. Friends who can be relied upon for warmth and cheer in times of despair: Poornima, Amit, Harsh, Satya, Sadiq, Mona, Inteshar, Imran, Mahmood, Anusha and Iqbal Ahmad.

Finally, my parents who put up with a negligent daughter, and Tanweer, for sharing my life, thank you.

Acronyms

ATS:	Anti-Terrorism Squad
CRPC:	Criminal Procedure Code
FIR:	First Information Report
HUJI:	Harkat-ul-Jihad-al-Islami
IM:	Indian Mujahideen
IPC:	Indian Penal Code
LET:	Lashkar-e Tayyaba
MCOCA:	Maharashtra Control of Organised Crime Act
NDA:	National Democratic Alliance
NSA:	National Security Advisor
NSCS:	National Security Council Secretariat
POTA:	Prevention of Terrorism Act
R&AW:	Research and Analysis Wing
SIMI:	Students' Islamic Movement of India
SPO:	Special Police Officer
STF:	Special Task Force
TADA:	Terrorist and Disruptive Activities (Prevention) Act
UAPA:	Unlawful Activities Prevention Act
UPA:	United Progressive Alliance

Preface

Once I had to drive a Mumbai ATS inspector across the city. He chatted about his B.A. degree (he too had studied Sociology), took an interest in my Ph.D. dissertation ("poor, young girls were initiated into nunhood"), recommended the SUV that zipped past us ("value for money"). But we were not out sight-seeing. In the rear seat was sitting a young man whose brother had been literally plucked by the ATS from the Delhi Police Special Cell, which he was helping track down some suspects. He was then charged with conspiring the July 2011 Zaveri bazar blast in Mumbai. The ATS had now come calling on *this* young man, to take him to Mumbai, ostensibly to 'question' him. But questioning often means warrantless arrests, illegal detention and torture leading to leaked stories in the media and charges of terrorism.

The ATS team had arrived in the middle of a press conference. This effectively frustrated their simple enough plan to carry away Nadeem[1] for uninterrupted interrogation in the comforts of their police station. Slightly

1 Name changed.

irritated at our presence, and shivering from the assault of the Delhi December cold, the Assistant Commissioner of Police (ACP) who headed the team began to inquire from this young man. The gist of his inquisition was this:

> "What did your brother tell the Special Cell?"
> "Wouldn't it be simpler to pose this question to the Special Cell?", we asked.
> "Protocol".

Apparently, the protocol is to whisk away suspects, or even their brothers.

So, now, here we were, discussing sociology, Jain nuns and large cars, headed towards Nadeem's house for a search, at the other end of the city.

> "Why do you illegally detain suspects?", I turned to a less pleasant topic. "How would it hurt to send summons to those you wish to interrogate?"
> The Inspector looked genuinely hurt. "Illegal detention? Never. We always take the person out for a walk after 23 hours."

It was one of those tragi-comic moments when one isn't sure whether to laugh or to cry. Here was an officer of law telling us that the legal requirement of producing an arrestee before a magistrate within 24 hours could be circumvented 'legally'.

This brief encounter was but a glimpse into the ease with which norms are institutionally subverted. It also gave us a first hand experience of the dread of being pursued. When every knock on the door, every ring of the phone makes your stomach churn; when the grey of the evening appears full of foreboding. But worst of all, the knowledge that no one may be able to help you from being taken away. The stories in Section I bear the imprint of this terror, felt as a visceral force. Some months after the above incident, I chanced upon a letter sent out by an accused in the Mumbai train bombings of 2006. The address was marked Anda Cell, Arthur Road prison. It was a grim chronicle of Ehtesham Qutub's 75-day-long custody in the ATS. One name leapt out of this letter of horror. It was the name of the Inspector.

He, who had amiably offered expert comments to me on my Ph.D. thesis, sympathizing with girls "who were tortured into becoming nuns," played a starring role in the letter as the master of ceremonies, conducting and executing a regimen of excruciating pain on the man under his power. This letter appears in "Dr. Narco and other Stories", which recounts the centrality of torture and cavalier prejudice in the Mumbai train blasts investigations. But this affliction is not unique to the Mumbai ATS; Section I shows these to be fundamental to all terror investigations: the Uttar Pradesh STF working on the Katcheri blasts of 2006, the Special Cell of Delhi Police which abducted the Intelligence Bureau (IB) informers and produced them in a dramatic press conference as Al Badr operatives; the Hyderabad Crime Branch – these agencies acting sometimes in collusion, at other times in competition, all tied tenuously by the shadowy IB.

Nothing compares to the fear of the early days. With time, however, the long arm of law manages to transform this palpable terror into a dull, unending ache. Section II explores the criminal justice framework of counterterrorism. Terror cases are prosecuted under the Unlawful Activities Prevention Act. Promulgated originally in 1967, the UAPA enabled the Centre to declare an organization as unlawful if it was of the opinion that the association "has become an unlawful association". Amended repeatedly since then, the ambit of 'unlawful' has been an ever-growing circle of acts and actors, strengthening the subjective basis of its application, virtually creating a suspicion state. Opposing Prevention of Terrorism Act (POTA) introduced by the NDA government, S Jaipal Reddy had laid out four grounds of objection to the legislation: "First, it is destructive of the basic democratic liberties; second, it has been demonstrated empirically in our own country that this is a remedy worse than the malady; third, it has been prompted, by malignant political motives; and fourth, it jettisons the basic established principles of criminal jurisprudence without a necessary protective shield."[2] However, the Parliament attack provided the NDA government an opportunity to push it through in a joint session of Parliment. Almost as a replay, the Mumbai attack in November 2008 drummed up support for a tough law against terror in the form of the amended Unlawful Activities Prevention Act (UAPA).

Short of admitting confession as evidence – to L.K. Advani's eternal irritation – the new, improved UAPA 2008 looked remarkably similar to Terrorist and Disruptive Activities (Prevention) Act (TADA) – which incidentally P Chidambaram had inaugurated in 1987 as Minister of State for Home. It extended the period of remand to 180 days while rendering the bail provisions extremely stringent. Appealing to his colleagues to pass the amended bill without insisting on a referral to the Standing Committee, Chidambaram assured them that Parliament could "revisit the Bills and make the improvements in course of time". Indeed, he promised, "If any improvements have to be done, we can always come back and look at the Bill when

---

2 S Jaipal Reddy, Lok Sabha Debates on approval of Prevention of Terrorism (Second) Ordinance, 2002, promulgated by the President on 18 March 2002.

we meet again in February."[3] The Parliament has only returned to the law to add more muscle to it.

In 2008, UAPA defined new offences such as terror funding and holding of terror camps, and voila you will suddenly find these charges surfacing in the FIRs – though with the sketchiest possible details. In 2013 the Parliament explicitly incorporated economic offences under the definition of terrorist acts. Amendment of Section 15 now declares the production, smuggling and circulation of "high quality counterfeit currency" as a terrorist offence, and not simply a financial one that was up till now dealt with under Sections 489B, 489C, 489D of the IPC. Punjab Police's partiality towards TADA's powerful provisions, or Maharashtra Police's quick recourse to Maharashtra Control of Organised Crime Act (MCOCA) over ordinary criminal law, has been too well documented to not know that police favour draconian laws when they are available.

What firmly entrenches UAPA into the slippery territory of conspiracy, intentions and 'knowledge', and away from specific, tangible and verifiable acts, is the introduction of a new section, which criminalizes the raising of funds "from a legitimate or illegitimate source... knowing that such funds are likely to be used ...by a terrorist organization"... "*notwithstanding whether such funds were actually used or not used*" for the commission of a terrorist act.[4] Knowledge that monies could be used

---

3 P Chidambaram, Combined discussion on the motion for consideration of the National Investigation Agency Bill, 2008 and the Unlawful Activities (Prevention) Amendment Bill, 2008. Bills passed on 17 December 2008.

4 For a detailed critique of the 2012 amendments to UAPA, see "Reject Amendments to UAPA: An Appeal to Members of the Rajya Sabha", Jamia Teachers' Solidarity Association, 4 December 2012; access at http://kafila.org/2012/12/04/reject-amend-

for terrorist acts will be difficult to prove in a court of law but it will effectively render suspect a variety of legal transactions: a movement raising funds to carry on its campaigns, a madrasa seeking contributions to rebuild its walls or replenish its library; or ageing parents receiving remittances from a child working overseas. Our police have only to suspect the people receiving monies for them to be put away in jails.

There is no study to prove that a tough law acts as deterrence against terrorism – howsoever one may choose to define the term. What we do have is ample evidence of such laws leading to gross violations of citizens' rights: illegal detentions, torture, false cases, long periods of incarceration – a wholesale recipe for 'disaffection', in fact. In the decade of its existence, 76,036 individuals were arrested for crimes under TADA. Of these, only one per cent ended in a conviction.[5] Similarly, at the time of its repeal, in 2004, 1031 persons were arrested under POTA. Trial was finally completed with regard to 18 of which 13 were convicted.[6] A national audit of UAPA trials and convictions is yet to be undertaken, but we do know that the investigating agencies dress up their conviction rates by

---

ments-to-uapa-an-appeal-to-members-of-the-rajya-sabha/; and "Passage of Amendments to UAPA: Further Erosion of Constitutional Rights", statement released by Jamia Teachers' Solidarity Association, 21 December 2012; access at http://www.teachers-solidarity.org/?q=node/110.

5 *Colonial Continuities: Human Rights, Terrorism and Security Laws in India* by Anil Kalhan, Gerald P. Conroy, Mamta Kaushal, Sam Scott Miller and Jed. S. Rakoff, *Columbia Journal of Asian Law* (20:1), 2005, p. 148. See Chapter IV "Contemporary Antiterrorism Laws".

6 Figures revealed by the former Home Minister Shivraj Patil on 11 May 2005. See "556 still detained under POTA: Patil", *Milli Gazette*, 16-30 June 2005.

including convictions under Arms Act or Explosive Substances Act under their terror conviction records.

Even as confessions are not admissible as evidence under UAPA, they are rather useful in constructing a mythology of guilt. Dossiers fattened on Interrogation Reports and disclosures have made the reputations of many national security experts. At least some essays in this collection are a direct response to the security commonsense of these experts. "Sinful Liberals and the Investigative Bias" is a retort to these experts who insist on the absence of prejudice in anti-terror investigations – that those acquitted by courts are not necessarily innocent and that investigative agencies are merely trying to go about their business, making a few wrong arrests in good faith. But more dangerously, the argument that in these times of terror, we should all agree to overlook the niceties of constitutional guarantees. Such a line of thought was propagated frenziedly in the press last year (2013) as the Central Bureau of Investigation (CBI) began to inquire into the truth behind the killing of Ishrat Jahan. "Why the Ishrat Jahan Case frightens our Commentators" was written in the middle of that maelstrom.

Though this collection of essays covers the period beginning 2001 – the year of 9/11, the Parliament attack, the ban on Students Islamic Movement of India (SIMI) – India's counterterrorism policies have a hoarier lineage. "Death by Encounter" attempts to trace the genealogy of extra-judicial killings, from the slaying of Naxalites during the Emergency, to KPS Gill's doctrine of rampant extermination in Punjab in the 1980s.

Every narrative has its milestones. The attack on Mumbai in 2008 – "India's 26/11" – occupies a preeminent place in the history of terrorism in India. From the debris of this attack arose the vision of a techno-security state, a new lexicon of homeland security imported from post-9/11 USA, and a new market for surveillance and security solutions. This vision of a hard State – with its tough anti-terror laws, an overarching national terrorism centre, invasive technologies of mapping and monitoring population – began to be pushed in earnest by the corporate world. Numerous reports and surveys by FICCI, CII, ASSOCHAM and consultancy firms on homeland security attest to the welding of ideological and material interests in this emerging security-industrial complex. Section III explores precisely this.

Part I

Stories from Kafkaland

Dr. Narco and Other Stories from Kafkaland

I. Action/Reaction

We are sipping our black coffees in silence. Me, just exhausted, and he killing time, before he is summoned into another TV studio. It's a busy day for 'security experts', the day after twin blasts in Hyderabad.[1] We have just finished a show where this gent has been on the whole sober, arguing that media and public pressure force agencies to commit errors. At this moment, the anchor strides in, and demands, "so, what is this Indian Mujahideen?"

"I was raring to answer this question – I wish you had asked me this. I have a theory on this" he says softly. As retired head of R&AW, he is expected to have a theory on this.

"I think Indian Mujahideen is a rubric. There are many cells, not connected with another." He continues, but it is instantly obvious that his theory is not original but the latest to emanate from the intelligence community.

---

1 The blasts occurred on 21 February 2013.

The honeycomb model of loose, uncoordinated cells, unrelated to each other is the favoured IM theory these days.

"I don't agree with Uday Bhaskar that the roots of IM are to be found in Babri Masjid or Gujarat 2002", referring to the argument of our co-panelist on the show.

Ok, here may be something interesting. "It goes back much farther."

"How far back? Independence? Partition? Pre-Independence?" ventures the anchor gamely.

"Oh no. Much farther back. It will be the subject of a rather long monologue, I'm afraid." But then undeterred by his own threat of monologue, he lowers his voice to a whisper. "Abrahamic traditions," he reveals, as though this may be a State secret. The sound of his own words has a warming effect on him. "There is no meeting ground between Abrahamic traditions and traditions of the east. Abrahamic traditions are history-centred unlike Hinduism."

He launches into a fusillade against Islam, forgetting for the moment, his own theory of Abrahamic traditions. "You see, jihad is a religious obligation in Islam."

"Hindus can *never* be violent," the Chief is in full flow now.

"What of the Mecca Masjid, Ajmer Sharif, Aseemanand, sadhvi Pragya?" asks the anchor. My head is oscillating between the two, almost as though this were a tennis match.

Chief smiles beatifically. "Hindus have been involved only in five incidents. These were *reactions* to what they saw around them. Hindu terrorism is an oxymoron. It *cannot* exist."

At this moment, I let out my breath, which I have been holding for the past five minutes, collect my bag and leave.

In January 2013, India's newsrooms suffered a collective implosion following the Home Minister's Jaipur blasphemy.[2] The Congress was left collecting the detritus as senior ministers dismissed Shinde's Hindu terror remarks as personal opinion. "Terror has no colour" became the sudden righteous slogan of all news channels and all regulars thereof. Have we ever termed jihadi terror as "green", they asked, incensed at the coinage of "saffron terror". The innocence of our experts was charming, if nothing else. Many cussed characters took a more uncharitable view of this hullabaloo over Hindu terror, but we can ignore these conspiracy theorists, for now. Let us focus for the moment on one of the favourites on the endless discussion programmes on news channels: a retired cop. A former police commissioner of Mumbai, MN Singh, who had led the investigations into the 'Black Friday' blasts of 1993 condemned it as "politically coined terminology... very handy for some people to counter the charge of jihadi terrorism." "In my opinion", he concluded, "there is nothing like Saffron terrorism. *It just doesn't exist in the Hindu pantheon*." (sic)

Sanatan Sanstha and Abhinav Bharat were localized phenomena, which had "been nipped in the bud" by the NIA. Terrorists of the Hindu variety – oxymoronic as they are, even if they exist – lack the capacity, the capability, the resources, but above all "*even the motivations*". Of course Mr. Singh did not rule out the possibility of involvement of some Hindu groups, but their actions were to be classed as "*retaliatory attacks*" – "retaliatory attacks

---

2 The then Home Minister Sushil Kumar Shinde speaking at the Congress Chintan Shivir at Jaipur said that his ministry had received reports that RSS had been promoting 'saffron terrorism' through training camps.

as opposed to organized home-grown terror sponsored by Pakistan".[3]

How could Hindus possibly bomb their own country – except in retaliation? The idea of Hindus as the only true and natural citizens of India has long been elevated to the mythical. As is the binary between a violent Islam and a non-violent Hinduism. These prejudices are the operating codes for those at the apex of investigating agencies. Frightening, but no longer surprising.

II. Mumbai

Suryaprakash. Sun light. Suggesting warmth, glow, life. But to those who have passed through the torture chambers of the Maharashtra ATS, it invokes horrific memories of burns, blisters and scorches – suffering which continues hours after suryaprakash oil is applied to their nostrils, anal passage and penis. Among these singularly unlucky men were those thirteen charged with planning and executing the blasts in Mumbai trains in 2006.

On 11th July 2006, in just over ten minutes, seven bombs tore through the first class compartments of Mumbai's local trains, killing close to 200 people and injuring hundreds others. In an act of cheap mimesis, commentators swiftly labeled it India's 7/11. In two days flat, the Home Ministry discovered SIMI's stamp over the blasts.[4]

A week after the blasts, the Mumbai Police released photos of two suspects, Sayyad Zabiuddin and Zulfeqar

---

3 For full video of the discussion, see http://www.ndtv.com/video/player/we-the-people/right-wing-terrorism-real-threat-or-overstated/265259?video-mostpopularEx-cop

4 "Mumbai blasts have SIMI stamp: Govt Agencies", *Indian Express*, 13 July 2006. expressindia.indianexpress.com/news/fullstory.php?newsid=70969

Fayyaz, and the following day, named a third one, Rahil.[5] Then slyly, only a week later, the same police presented three catches to the media: Kamal Ansari and Khalid Aziz Ronak Sheikh arrested from Basupatti village in Madhubani district of Bihar; Ansari's brother-in-law Mumtaz Ahmed Maqbool Ahmed Choudhary from Navi Mumbai.[6]

Neither the Mumbai police, nor the crime reporters remembered anything about the first list of suspects.

Between July and September, many more arrests were made, taking the total to 13, and the crime was triumphantly declared as solved. At a press conference, held on 30 September, the Commissioner of Police described the ATS's handiwork as a "beautiful piece of highly professional investigation"[7] and outlined how ISI had trained, supported and directed Lashkar and SIMI operatives to carry out the blasts, working in pairs. He also described in precise detail how the bombs were rigged: From RDX sourced from Pakistan and locally available ammonium nitrate, one Mohammad Ali fashioned these bombs, packing the explosives into "eight five litre pressure cookers of the brand name Kanchan".[8]

By way of proving the ISI-SIMI collaboration, a dead body lying unclaimed in the city morgue was identified

---

5 "Mumbai Blasts: Hunt is on for Rahil", *Times of India*, 14 July 2006. Access at: http://articles.timesofindia.indiatimes.com/2006-07-14/india/27791686_1_serial-blasts-rdx-explosives-mumbai-police-commissioner

6 "Arrested trio were in touch with bomb-makers in Mumbai" by Sagnik Chowdhury, *Indian Express*, 24 July 2006. http://www.indianexpress.com/news/arrested-trio-were-in-touch-with-bomb-makers-in-mumbai/9161/

7 "How Mumbai Police Cracked 7/11 Case", available at http://ibnlive.in.com/news/how-police-cracked-7-11-case/22900-3.html

8 http://www.liveindia.com/news/zzzs.html

as Salim from Lahore.[9] This dead man was listed in the chargesheet as deceased accused 1, address and other details not known, nationality Pakistani. No one asked, and none answered as to how a burnt and mangled torso wrenched out from the blast site was identified as 'Salim of Lahore, other details not known'.

News reports from that period – based largely on official press conferences, which are always aplenty in Mumbai, and unofficial sources, which never run dry anywhere – describe how the case was cracked. Even then, it would have been obvious to any half caring observer, there wasn't much. The case hinged primarily on two things: telephone records; and secondly, in admitted absence of other evidences and leads, the 'scientific method' of narco-analysis.[10]

Lets look at the telephone records first. The breakthrough in the case allegedly came from high traffic of phone calls between Mumtaz and his brother-in-law Kamal Ansari in the week preceding the blasts. The duo's guilt hinged on the reference to Nepal – which is in touching distance of Ansari's Madhubani village, and which every Bihari in that belt will tell you is the favoured destination for weekly shopping.

Between 17 August and 25 September 2006, the ATS filed five remand applications seeking the custody of accused on grounds that their cell phones had been seized and their call records were being obtained, compared and analyzed.

A remand application, dated 22 August 2006, claimed that Abdul Wahid Din Shaikh (accused 8) used to give his

---

9 Report in Deutsche Presse-Agentur, 30 September 2006. http://rawstory.com/news/2006/Pakistan_s_ISI_involved_in_Mumbai_t_09302006.html

10 http://ibnlive.in.com/news/how-police-cracked-7-11-case/22900-3.html

mobile phone for "contacting members of *LashkareToiba* outside India" on behalf of Mohammad Sajid Ansari (accused 7).

An extension of the remand of accused 1-9 was sought on the claim that Kamal Ansari had received arms training in Pakistan and "used the mobile phone and email addresses for communicating with those persons (in Pakistan) and passing on message. The call records of his mobile phone are being analyzed." This was on 25 September. On the same day, ATS filed another application listing recoveries of cell phones and sim cards from Dr. Tanveer (accused 2), Ehtesham Kutubuddin Siddiqui (accused 4), Shaikh Mohammad Ali Alam Shaikh (accused 6), which had been sent to the FSL Hyderabad "for examining and extracting information in it." It also stated "that on the instructions from the accused No. 5 Mohd. Faizal, the accused No. 6 was contacting other members of LeT on his mobile phone of a given number."[11]

Each remand application created the impression of hectic investigations and forensics whose fruitful conclusion necessitated extended periods of remand. Not one of these applications was turned down. From the time of their detention to the press conference on 30 September, all 13 remained in the custody of the ATS. But apparently, this rich haul of evidence by way of CDRs were to be supplemented by the 'scientific' method of narco analysis, which would supposedly reveal the modus operandi of the operatives: how they went to Pakistan for training; how they helped the Pakistani operatives to cross over to India; how they prepared the bombs and planted them, down to the minutest detail.

---

11 Remand applications cited in judgement passed by the High Court of Bombay in the Criminal Appeals 973 and 992/2012 in the MCOC Special Case 21 of 2006. Dated 10 Dec. 2012. Copy on record.

On the second anniversary of the blasts in 2008, Shahid Azmi, lawyer for the train blasts accused, himself later felled by the bullets of hired assassins, circulated two letters on behalf of the accused.[12] The first was a letter of condolence to the victims of the blasts. "We, thirteen – innocent accused, are with you in this time of the grief and remembrance," it said.

> We request you not to consider us as murderers, but victims who are suffering for a deed with which they have no connection at all. We are not a part of any conspiracy, nor are we associated in any way with Lashkar-e Tayyaba. We have not even seen any al-Qaeda manual, we are not bomb makers nor are we the planters. To be true we have not committed any crime nor have we given any confession.
>
> ATS has just played this game with the sole aim of silencing the public and the so called leaders and to diffuse the atmosphere of fear that had been created. Unfortunately, the perpetrators of the terror are still roaming free. The truth is that the ATS remained clueless (intentionally or unintentionally) and we were made the scapegoats so that they heave a sigh of relief. No doubt you are suffering for the loss of your near and dear ones, but we are suffering each moment for the last two years.

The second letter titled 'Arrest of the Accused – the Real Facts' chronicled in chilling and bare prose the diverse practices of cruelty devised by the ATS. Tied to a plank with ropes, water is poured continually on the face till the chosen victim loses consciousness – meanwhile a machine monitors blood pressure to ensure that it doesn't spike up too high, causing death. Trussed up in a chair, unable to move his head even an inch, the victim is subjected to a continuous falling of water droplets. Hours of this unceasing torture lead to severe pain in neck and head. Legs torn asunder at 180 degrees, gases which cause painful

12 E Mail received on 22 November 2008. Copy on record.

swelling of the body, high voltage shocks to private parts, beatings by flour mill belts, humiliation and stripping of family members – it's a sickening catalogue guaranteed to make your bile rise; torture that broke them psychologically but also left its imprint on the bodies of these men. But not enough apparently for the magistrate – to whom the accused even submitted a written complaint about the torture inflicted upon them – to act to ensure their safety. Disregarding the written submission, the court extended their custody to the ATS who renewed their brutalization with greater vigour. No doubt, the bogey of CDR analysis was crucial to these extraordinarily long remands.

Two years after Shahid Azmi circulated the letter to civil rights activists, and just months after he was assassinated, the venerable editor of *Milli Gazette* received a letter from the high security Anda Cell of Mumbai Central Jail. The writer of this letter was Ehtesham Qutub, accused number 4 in the Mumbai train blasts case. It described in detail not only the tools and devices of torture in the various offices of ATS and Mumbai police, but also the farce of narco analysis, conducted without consent of the accused, or permission from the court. Ehtesham was subjected to the first test in Chandan Chowki at Juhu on 5 August 2006 in the presence of officers from Forensic Science Laboratory (FSL), Mumbai.[13]

The next day, Ehtesham writes, he was taken to Bangalore for brain mapping, polygraph and narco analysis test through a Jet Airways flight. He was subjected to these tests a third time on 12 September 2006, and yet again on 24 September. In Bangalore, these tests were conducted by Dr. Malini, the institute's Assistant Director, notorious as 'Dr. Narco'. Ehtesham wasn't the only one to be

---

13 The letter was published in *Milli Gazette* as 'My 75 Days of Horror in the Hands of ATS'. http://www.milligazette.com/print/issue/1-15-october-2010

injected with sodium pentathol, a banned drug, used as anaesthesia in these tests, and which can cause heart attack – all accused suffered these degrading tests multiple times. What information did the ATS extract from these tests? This was revealed when the ATS confronted the accused with a CD of these sessions. Whilst these dubious tests have no validity – inadmissible in court as evidence – the accused were stunned to discover that the tapes had been manipulated and questions inserted to produce a narrative of guilt. For example:

> Q: How many bombs were planted?
> A: Seven
>
> The original question had been:
> Q: What comes after six?
> A: seven
>
> Q: Who was involved in the conspiracy of the blasts?
> A: Dr. Tanveer, Ehtesham, Faisal, Kamal Muzammil, Asif.
>
> The original question was:
> Q: Who are the people in the cells next to yours?
> A: Dr. Tanveer, Ehtesham, Faisal, Kamal Muzammil, Asif.

Ehtesham, in his letter from prison, accused Dr. Malini of colluding with the ATS to produce these doctored CDs. In the second letter sent out by Azmi in 2008, Naveed, accused number 12, complained that Dr. Malini forced favourable answers out of him by pulling his ears with a plier as he lay drugged and vulnerable in her lab. These cannot be dismissed as empty allegations of men frustrated by long years of incarceration. In his prison diaries, published after he was acquitted of charges of being a treasonous Naxalite, Arun Ferreira recounted his tryst with Dr. Malini: "During narco-analysis, she slapped and abused me, pinched my ears with pliers, and even administered electric shocks to me and my co-accused to keep us from turning unconscious."[14] When she was ignominiously ousted in 2009, there were 400 cases in queue waiting for her expert attention, a reflection of her reputation for 'results' amongst investigating agencies.[15]

What is clear now, but should have been obvious at that time too, was that the charade of CDRs was being played out to buy time. Time needed to torture and extract confessions. The narco tests provided a template for the confessions – for this is all that the prosecution's shaky scaffolding stood on. These torture confessions were all that held up the weight of the 11,000-page chargesheet. So when the accused retracted their confessions, alleging that they had been extracted through torture, they were brutally attacked inside the Mumbai Central Prison. A judicial inquiry submitted to the High Court, indicted not only the jail officials but also the doctors of the government hospital for participating in falsifying evidence of

---

14 "Prison Diaries" by Arun Ferreira, *Open* Magazine, 16 June 2012. http://www.openthemagazine.com/article/nation/prison-diaries

15 Dr. Malini was sacked from her post and job amidst allegations that she had forged her certificates to acquire the position that wasn't even officially sanctioned – and one that she didn't qualify for, as she wasn't a psychiatrist. By then, many of her results had come under a cloud. The Kerala High Court had rejected her findings in the famous Sister Abhaya case; there were sordid rumours that she leaked recordings of the narco tests to favoured television channels. See "Dr. Narco's Gone: What will Happen to the Cases", *Rediff.com*, 27 February 2009. http://www.rediff.co.in/news/2009/feb/27narco-what-will-happen-to-narco-cases-after-malinis-ouster.htm. Also see "Fake Documents: Government sacks FSL's Dr. Malini" by Hemanth Kumar, *DNA*, 26 February 2009. http://www.dnaindia.com/bangalore/report_fake-documents-govt-sacks-fsls-dr-malini_1234310

attack on the inmates by deliberately failing to maintain records of injuries and refusing to treat the injured and bleeding prisoners.[16]

The voluminous chargesheet itself is an interesting document: the pressure cookers – down to the brand – announced with such fanfare as the containers of the bombs disappeared mysteriously from the chargesheet. "Evidence has come on record," it now reads, "that on 10.07.2006 after the explosive devices were assembled and kept in *black Rexene bags*; this very place was used by the conspirators to store the explosive devices before they were brought to Churchgate Railway Station on 11.07.2006."

The call details, once deemed so crucial necessitating endless extensions of custody of the accused, are not so much as mentioned in the chargesheet. In November 2009, when the prosecution evidence was being adduced, Ehtesham Qutub moved an application in the trial court seeking the CDRs of the telephones of the accused pleading that these would prove the innocence of the accused. The Special Public Prosecutor pleaded, "the prosecution was required to furnish the accused with the copies of only those documents that are relied upon by the prosecution, and that the application be dismissed." Dismissing the application, the court passed an order: "I do not consider that production of the documents asked for is necessary or desirable for the purpose of trial before this Court."

One year later, Kamal Ansari, accused number 1, appealed to the trial court to direct the ATS to submit the CDRs of his mobile phone collected by the agency during the investigation as he was certain that the records would

---

16 Report of Inquiry No. 1 in the High Court Writ Petitions 1377 and 1496 of 2008. Conducted by Shri TV Nalawade, the Principal Judge, City Civil and Sessions Court, submitted on 13 October 2008. Copy on record.

support the "defence of alibi". Again, the SPP scoffed at this appeal urging the court to turn it down once again. The court agreed with the SPP that prosecution was duty bound to supply only those documents on which it has relied.

It was the High Court that finally said that whether those documents were relied upon by the prosecution or not "was an irrelevant consideration" if the accused felt that it could help "prove their innocence or facilitate their defence".

In fact it asked why the prosecution consistently stonewalled all appeals for the production of the records: "Was the prosecution conceding that these documents would establish what the appellants claimed they would? If not, what was the objection to produce the same and disprove the claim of appellants that the same would establish their innocence? Was the prosecution suggesting, by objecting to the production thereof, that if anything in favour of the accused had been found as a result of investigation, they were entitled to hide it and would not show it even to the Court?"[17]

Faced with a court that refused to buy the shallowness of the plea that the prosecution will not produce what wasn't relied upon, the ATS lobbed a new grenade: it simply did not have the records. The telecom companies also initially tried wriggling out by feigning lack of records; and then demanded Rs 34 lakh to ferret them out. Only in March 2013 did they begin to furnish the CDRs free of cost[18] – six years after the police claimed that these

---

17 Criminal appeal numbers 973&992-12; *Kamal Ahmed Mohammed Vakil and Others vs State of Maharashtra*, High Court of Bombay; Abhay M Thipsay, J., 10 December 2012.

18 "7/11 Blasts Case: Telecoms agree to give CDRs for free", *Indian Express*, 7 March 2013. http://www.indianexpress.com/news/711-blasts-case-telecom-firms-agree-to-give-cdrs-for-free/1084282

call records held the key to unraveling the conspiracy, and three years after the accused demanded these be placed on record.

Such is the machinery of our criminal justice system: investigators who torture; doctors who comply; pseudo-scientists with dubious truth serums; judges who ignore signs of torture; and a media which carries the burden of national security on its frail shoulders.

The Life and Death of Gulam Yazdani

There are two ways in which to recreate the short life of Gulam Yazdani, or Naveed as he was called at home. The first relies on IB dossiers, interrogation reports and news reports based on the first two. In this narrative, Yazdani appears as an engineering student who turned to a life of terrorism and met his well-deserved end at the hands of the police in 2006. A native of Nalgonda, Yazdani was said to have been among the 14 men from the state who were recruited to be trained by the Lashkar in Pakistan after the Gujarat riots. Alleged mastermind of the Dilsukhnagar Saibaba temple blast in 2002, Haren Pandya murder in 2003 and suicide attack on STF Headquarters in Hyderabad in 2005, the bombing of Delhi Patna Shramjeevi Express at Jaunpur in 2005, Yazdani quickly rose to head the Lashkar's South India operation and was among the most wanted men on the Andhra Pradesh police list. He had also allegedly hatched a plan to blow up a Ganesh temple near Secunderabad railway station.[1]

1 For typical stories, see "Yazdani belonged to Nalgonda" by S Ramu, 9 March 2006, *The Hindu*; "The story of LeT's south India chief" by Syed Amin Jafri in Hyderabad, 16 March 2006,

And then there is a more complex plot. Leave for the moment, these secret documents and look at the court records. In late 1999, Manik Prabhu Medical Stores, owned by a RSS worker, witnessed a shootout, leaving the owner's brother, Devender, dead. An FIR was lodged in the Saidabad police station.[2] The New Year brought the Task Force to Gulam Yazdani's house. He was taken away but not produced before a magistrate. Precisely a month after Yazdani had been disappeared, he was formally arrested by the Saidabad police.

The investigation was transferred to CID in the month of May. The new agency booked a completely different set of accused – among them, Syed Maqbool, in the news following the Dilsukhnagar blasts of 2013, for revealing that the area was on the target of terrorists.[3]

In the period when Yazdani was in the custody of Task Force, two more cases were slapped against him: in the first, which was also transferred to the CID, Yazdani was charged with conspiracy and waging war against the nation; in the second, lodged just a day before he was produced in court, the police showed recoveries of detonators and pistols, and booked him under Arms Act and Explosive Substances Act.[4] Released on bail, Yazdani was ultimately discharged from the Devender murder case and acquitted in the other two cases.

Rediffnews. http://www.rediff.co.in/news/2006/mar/16let.htm. "The Well-Tempered Jihad: the politics and practice of post-2002 Islamist terrorism in India" by Praveen Swami, *Contemporary South Asia*, 16:3, 2008, 303-322.

2 Crime No. 195/1999, Saidabad PS.

3 http://ibnlive.in.com/news/full-text-delhi-police-interrogation-report-on-ims-recce-of-dilsukh-nagar/374369-62-127.html

4 Crime No. 1/2000, Saidabad PS and Crime No. 33/2000, Saidabad PS.

It is not clear how Yazdani came to be called the architect of the Haren Pandya murder but in circles whose denizens go by the label of 'security experts', this has become an article of faith. Yazdani, in fact, is not named an accused in the Haren Pandya murder case.

In the years following the 2002 Gujarat pogrom, the cult of the *Hindu hriday samrat* was being carefully crafted. The numerous conspiracies 'detected' against Narendra Modi were crucial in fashioning the principal Hindutva icon and cementing the loyalties of his followers.

This was the period when police and investigating agencies in Gujarat claimed to have foiled a series of potential assassination attempts on Narendra Modi by liquidating 'terrorists'.[5] Registry of POTA cases also surged: all those booked under POTA were Muslims accused of either plotting to kill BJP leaders or conspiring to terrorize Hindus of Gujarat.[6]

The most gargantuan of these was the Gujarat ISI Conspiracy Case, more popularly known as the DCB 6 case, registered in April 2003, a month after Haren Pandya was killed. It had a mammoth list of over 80 accused – a list which kept swelling well after the chargesheets had been filed, and POTA had been repealed.[7] Yazdani was at home when news of Hyderabad boys being herded to Gujarat in the DCB 6 case started appearing. Similar

---

5 For an exhaustive list, see Amnesty Document, *India: A Pattern of Unlawful Killings by the Gujarat Police, Urgent Need for Effective Investigations*, AI Index: ASA 20/011/2007 (Public).

6 See 'Production of Terrorists Act' by Mukul Sinha for a full list of POTA cases in Gujarat. http://nsm.org.in/2008/09/29/pota-production-of-terrorist-act/

7 "ISI conspiracy case keeps draconian law alive in Gujarat", TNN 24 Nov. 2004. http://articles.timesofindia.indiatimes.com/2004-1124/ahmedabad/27156186_1_conspiracy-case-pandya-murder-hn-jhalaTOI.

conspiracy cases were filed in Andhra against all those implicated in the DCB 6. Two cases in Nalgonda district were registered against Yazdani where he was declared 'absconding accused'.[8] One evening, Yazdani did not return home. About fifteen days later, his father, the old Gulam Mustafa, received a call from him. Yazdani said he had fled to escape being ensnared in yet another case. He refused to divulge his location for fear that he would be arrested.

"I never saw my brother after that", Gulam Rabbani tells me over phone, "We only saw his dead body."

We do not know what he did in those intervening years. How he lived, where he lived. We will never know perhaps. The intelligence reports say he rose to prominence in the Lashkar ranks, planning, for example, the suicide attack on STF headquarters in Hyderabad. Did he? A man with backpack walked into the deserted STF headquarters – Dussehra eve keeping most STF personnel away from office – and blew himself up. His severed head and torso were recovered from outside the office. How he was identified as Mohtasin Bilal, a Bangladeshi national, carrying out the HUJI-B's first such operation,[9] is itself interesting. From the charred debris of this human bomb, investigators recovered a suicide note,[10], and a rubber slipper with a tell-all price tag that read 'Taka 100'.[11]

---

8 One Town Police Station and Narkepalli Poilce Station. These were also cases of sedition, including Sections 120 B, 121, 121 A, 124 A, 153 A, 153 B etc.

9 "Well-Tempered Jihad" by Swami, p. 309.

10 "Human Bomb in Andhra", *Telegraph*, Friday, 14 October 2005. http://www.telegraphindia.com/1051014/asp/nation/story_5352734.asp

11 "Terror's southern gateway" by Neena Gopal, *Gulf News*, 9 February 2006. http://gulfnews.com/opinions/columnists/terror-s-southern-gateway-1.224519

These clues, salvaged extraordinarily from the burnt body disclosed to the investigators his identity!

"Two and half month's later, on December 27, 2005," we learn, "three HuJI-B militants involved in the Hyderabad attack were arrested by the Special Cell of the Delhi police."[12] Less than two weeks later, Deputy NSA Vijay Nambiar and NSCS Additional Secretary SD Pradhan met US' Deputy Chief of Mission in Delhi, Robert Blake to "pledge to seek the NSA's approval for greater intelligence sharing on terrorism threats within India." The discussion fixated on terror threats in the South. Blake in his confidential cable dispatch that day wrote:

> Pradhan also noted that the terrorists themselves are different and more adaptable. For example, 'Arshad,' who was arrested on December 18 in connection with the October 12 suicide attack on the Hyderabad Police Special Task Force office, was a police informer who benefited from a police security escort.[13]

Interrogation reports made their way into expert commentary and created mounting evidence of Yazdani's guilt:

> Previously in August 2005, police had arrested Mohammad Ibrahim, a resident of Hyderabad, who revealed details of his travels in Bangladesh in 2004, his meetings with Ghulam Yazdani, the person involved in the Hiren Pandya murder in Gujarat on March 23, 2003, and his encounters with several HuJI terrorists from India and Pakistan. Four months before his arrest, in April 2005, Ibrahim had been sent to Karachi on

---

12 "HUJI: Lengthening Shadow of Terror" by Bibhu Prasad Routray, *SAIR* 31/7/06 1 August 2006. http://www.satp.org/satporgtp/sair/Archives/5_3.htm

13 "D/nsa Supports Intel Sharing On Terrorism; Says Terror In South Not New But Tactics And Targets Are"; 9 January 2006, Confidential Section 01 OF 06 New Delhi 000161. Accessed at: http://wikileaks.org/cable/2006/01/06NEWDELHI161.html

> a Bangladeshi passport, from where he was taken to an ISI camp in Balochistan.[14]

Mohammad Ibrahim had been arrested on charges of conspiracy and sedition.[15] In November 2005, Yazdani's brother, then a first year student of MCA at Osmania University PG College at Saidabad, was arrested in the case, charged with financially supporting Mohammad Ibrahim in his terrorist activities. He learnt later that he had been declared an 'absconder' even as he was attending classes at his college. In 2009, the First Additional Metropolitan Magistrate acquitted both Ibrahim and Yazdani's brother of all charges, as the prosecution could bring forth no evidence to substantiate the charges.[16] Meanwhile, however, Gulam Rabbani's arrest added to the legend of the "dreaded absconder" Yazdani.[17]

Yazdani's father's impassioned plea to his son to return home in January 2006 at the office of the then ACP Rajiv Trivedi was widely reported in the press. In the following

---

14 "HUJI: Lengthening Shadow of Terror" by Bibhu Prasad Routray, *SAIR* 31/7/06. 1 August 2006. http://www.satp.org/satporgtp/sair/Archives/5_3.htm

15 Crime No. 234/2005, Gopalapuram PS, Secunderabad.

16 Sessions Case No. 192 of 2006, Judgement pronounced by Shri Sreeram Murthy, First Additional Metropolitan Magistrate, 12 November 2007. See also, "Court lets off 3 in conspiracy case", TNN 13 November 2007, http://articles.timesofindia.indiatimes.com/2007-11-13/hyderabad/27976059_1_conspiracy-case-delhi-police-office-bomb-blast-case. Rabbani's experience in the interrogation room left him a changed man. Upon receiving bail, he quit his MCA and enrolled in a law college, and is today a practicing lawyer. Personal conversation.

17 See for example, "Yazdani belonged to Nalgonda", *The Hindu*, op. cit. Also, 'Nalgonda supplies 'terrorists' in hordes' by Koride Mahesh, TNN, 10 March 2006. http://articles.timesofindia.indiatimes.com/2006-03-10/hyderabad/27824815_1_nalgonda-isi-activities-terrorist-activities.

month, Gulam Mustafa received a call from Trivedi. He enquired about Yazdani's physical features and identification marks, and very specifically, if he spoke haltingly. When Mustafa confirmed this, he was advised to forget about Yazdani and focus on the other sons. Trivedi's words, says the family, appeared ominous to them even then. On the evening of 7 March, three bombs exploded in Varanasi. The next morning, news agencies flashed the encounter killing of Yazdani and another man at the hands of the Special Cell of the Delhi Police. "Lashkar terrorists" had been gunned down in the early hours of the morning in Bawana, the last outpost of Delhi.[18]

This is how a Delhi Police press release announcing gallantry awards for the architect of the encounter described the encounter:

> Information was received that 2 Let militants namely Ghulam Yezdani and Kajol would be arriving at Alipur Narela Road, Holambi Kalan T Point on 8.3.06. Police team headed by ACP Sanjeev kumar Yadav along with Inspector Mohan Chand Sharma reached Alipur Narela Road and took positions at the strategic points. When terrorists reached the spot, ACP Sanjeev Yadav and Inspector Mohan Chand Sharma disclosed the identity of the police team and asked the militants to surrender. Both the militants were later on identified as Ghulam Yazdani @ Naved … Ahsan Ullah Hasan @ Kabab Mohd @ Shahbaz Mohd @ Sajid Mehmood @ Shumon @ Jamil @ Ahmed @ Kajol r/o Chorangi Mor, Jheelchuli, Faridpur, Bangladesh. The militants did not pay to the heed and started firing at the approaching police party. ACP Sanjeev Yadav without caring for their life, faced hail of bullets fired by terrorist Ahsan Ullah Hasan @ kajol and gave chase to him. The militant was constantly and indiscriminately firing towards him. Unfazed and undeterred Sh. Sanjeev Kumar Yadav in self defence and in order to apprehend the militants returned fire and shot dead Kajol. Inspector Mohan

18 "Two LeT Ultras shot dead in Delhi Encounter", 8 March 2006, PTI. Accessed at: http://news.outlookindia.com/items.aspx?artid=368758

> Chand Sharma on the other hand was facing indiscriminate firing from other militant Yezdani who had taken position behind a wall in the field. Inspector Sharma crawled on the road without caring for bodily injuries and took position so that the militant could not take the benefit of boundary wall. During exchange of fire the militant was shot dead.
>
> Recognizing gallant act, ACP Sanjeev Kumar Yadav has been conferred President Police Medal for Gallantry while Late Inspector Mohan Chand Sharma has been awarded 1st Bar to President's Police Medal for Gallantry. (sic)[19]

This sparse prose is the template for almost all encounter killings in Delhi. Only the names of the victims change.

The family says that the body bore marks of torture, there were deep holes as though he had been drilled into and the head was misshapen. In the absence of a post mortem report, and the reluctance of the Delhi Police to hand over Yazdani's body to the family, despite a High Court order directing them to do so, is there any reason to disbelieve them? [20]

Let us return briefly to Syed Maqbool. A small news item, which has not rivaled the popularity of his interrogation report leaked by Delhi Police, quotes 'sources' to say that Maqbool had become a police informant after his acquittal in the Devender murder case, and that his arrest was a consequence of rivalry between Delhi Police and

---

19 "Gallantry Awards to Delhi Police Personnel" (Delhi Police Press Release; 25 January 2009). delhipolice.nic.in/home/backup/25-01-2009.doc

20 "Encounter victim's kin stage dharna, seek CBI probe" by Omer Farooq, *Pioneer*, 8 May 2007. Reproduced at: **http://www.indiarightsonline.com/Sabrang/relipolcom16.nsf/5e7647d942f529c9e5256c3100376e2e/d9fa52a5d7ec4c03652572f00044105f?OpenDocument**. Also personal conversation with family.

Maharshtra ATS.[21] Recall also Pradhan's frank admission to the US Deputy Chief of Mission that the accused in the STF attack was a police informer. Did persistent implication in terror cases push Yazdani to seek refuge with groups he was accused of being associated with? Did the police force him to turn informer for them? Was Yazdani used cynically by agencies and then disposed off when it suited them? Was he already in the custody of one agency or another when the telephone call was made to his father? These are not answers likely to emerge from the dossiers of the IB, reproduced endlessly till they acquire the sanctity of truth.

In this opaque netherland of terrorism-counterterrorism, it is not just loyalties that change side, but entire sides which overturn and mirror each other in grotesque ways. The good guys battling the evil ones is a fantasy manufactured by think tanks and the experts industry. In the confidential dispatch that Blake sent home, he quoted Nambiar's assurance to him that the author of "Behind Bangalore: The Origins of the Long Jihad",[22] had "obviously has been briefed, most likely by the Intelligence Bureau (IB)."

---

21 See "Murder accused spilled the beans on Indian Mujahideen recce", TNN 23 February 2013. http://articles.timesofindia.indiatimes.com/2013-02-23/hyderabad/37256650_1_delhi-police-begum-bazaar-land-dispute

22 Praveen Swami, 9 January 2006, http://www.hindu.com/2006/01/09/stories/2006010904441000.htm

Terrorism's True Lies

There is a fairly typical kind of story that appears in the media after every bomb blast. It is accompanied by a visual spread which graphically 'joins the dots' in the supposed Indian terror network, the Indian Mujahideen. At the centre of this graphic is Atif Amin, the youth slain in the 'encounter' at Batla House, and various arrows shoot out towards photos of 'Bhatkal brothers', mufti Abu Bashar, an elusive Abdul Subhan Qureshi 'Tauqeer' and many others. The cast changes marginally, and the plot moves between Kerala, Bhatkal in Karnataka, Azamgarh in Uttar Pradesh, Ujjain and Khandwa in Madhya Pradesh with detours into Hyderabad, Maharashtra and Gujarat.

SIMI, IM, Lashkar, HuJI morph seamlessly into each other in this story of homegrown terror. Speaking at the launch of a book, titled unimaginatively, *Indian Mujahideen: The Enemy Within* (2011), to an audience made up largely of the elite of the security and intelligence establishment, the then Home Minister Chidambaram stressed that we could no longer rest easy in the assumption that the source of terror was across the border – we must wake up to the home grown variety that SIMI and IM represent. The author, described glowingly by Arun Jaitley, the other speaker at the book launch as a "foot-soldier", does a stunning regurgitation of chargesheets and confessions – the latter not even admissible in court. This book was launched around the time two prominent magazines chose to do cover stories on the Indian Mujahideen[1] (based again on chargesheets and confessions and little else), weeks after the blasts in Mumbai – and barely a month after the investigative agencies were claiming successes in busting modules and making arrests. The month of June saw several arrests in Madhya Pradesh – even a shootout in Ratlam in which ostensibly high-ranking IM operatives were arrested – and the Gujarat police claimed the trophy of alleged IM man, Danish Reyaz.

Does the IM exist? If it does, what precisely is it? In all honesty, it's not a question that is easy to answer – given that the only proofs of the existence of the organization have been the e-mails received after the 2008 blasts, and the State dossiers. The arrest of Yasin Bhatkal in August 2013 unleashed another round of fierce and frenzied reporting – with his disclosures and confessions claiming the omnipresent IM hand everywhere, making headlines each day. What can be done – and ought to be done by journalists who love the prefix 'investigative' – is to subject the police and anti-terror agencies claims to some scrutiny, especially so after Malegaon and Mecca Masjid revelations. Such an exercise reveals another pattern altogether: this is the web spun by agencies of counterterrorism, whose threads connect between Kashmir and Delhi Special Cell, the Gujarat ATS and the Uttar Pradesh ATS, and various police departments in between.

---

1 The Terror, The Threat. The Twist", *Tehelka*, Vol. 8, Issue 30, 30 July 2011 and "IM-Printed..." *Outlook*, 1 August 2011.

Investigating agencies are predisposed towards 'picking up' suspects and accused far ahead of the arrest shown in FIRs, chargesheets and media conferences and leaks. The phrase 'picking up' reflects our unique ability to sanitize and blunt the jagged edges of investigative process to which illegal detention is crucial – just as 'encounters' are a glamorous and Bollywoody euphemism for cold-blooded executions. This is now so routine that it's lost all novelty. Take the case of Qamar and Irshad Ali, kidnapped by the Special Cell of the Delhi Police in December 2005 and then declared arrested while alighting from a Kashmir Roadways bus in February 2006, full two months after they were disappeared. It turned out in the end that Qamar and Irshad were not operatives of Al Badar, as the Special Cell claimed, but IB informers who fell out of favour when they refused to carry out the directives of their bosses.

Or consider the case of Md. Sarwar, one of the key accused in the Jaipur blasts of 2008. A B.Tech from Integral University, Lucknow, Sarwar arrived in mid January 2009 to work in the Ujjain branch of a Hyderabad-based IT company. On the evening of 19 January 2009, four days after he had joined work, when he stepped out of the premises, he did not return. When he failed to return the next day, his office filed a missing persons complaint at the Neelganga police station, Ujjain, and were told that in all probability the police had taken him away. On 22 January, two days after a missing persons complaint had been filed in Ujjain, Sarwar's family received a call from Lucknow ATS that their son had been arrested from Lucknow in connection with Jaipur blasts.

Abu Bashar, a cleric from Beenapara, Azamgarh, charged with indoctrinating young IM recruits to wage jihad, was picked up in full public view from his home on 14 August 2008 by half a dozen men in plainclothes, following which his father rushed to the Sarai Meer police station, fearing abduction. He was rebuffed and no effort was made by the local police to trace the missing mufti. The local papers though were agog with this story and some quoted the Superintendent of Police, Azamgarh as saying that Bashar was a SIMI activist and had been arrested by the ATS. These stories appeared on the 15 August – surprise then that the ATS announced on 16 August that they had arrested Abu Bashar from outside the Charbagh railway station in Lucknow earlier that day at dawn.

Truth didn't hurt anybody, believes the UP ATS, as did its predecessor, the Special Task Force (STF). On 12 December 2007, after serial blasts rocked courts in Faizabad, Barabanki and Lucknow on 23 November, the STF abducted Tariq, a traditional practitioner of medicine who was on his way to an international *ijtema* (religious gathering) being organized by Tablighi Jamaat. Hakim Tariq was in charge of the health camp at the *ijtema*. While crossing the Mahmoodpur checkpost in Rani ki Sarai (Azamgarh), his bike was waylaid by a group of men aboard a white jeep. When others present on the spot opposed what they perceived to be a kidnapping, they were told that it was a family dispute and Tariq was only being returned home, which he had left after a tiff. Between 13 and 20 December, a missing persons complaint was filed, an application moved in the court of the chief judicial magistrate; the District Information Office was asked if it had any information about the whereabouts of Tariq; local residents organized protests and demonstrations demanding that Tariq be produced before the court. The news of Tariq's disappearance was widely covered in the local press.

On 16 December, Khalid Mujahid, a recently married teacher at a local girls' madrasa, was sent out to buy *neel* (indigo). But when he reached the market, the savouries of Munnu Chaat Bhandar tempted him. As he stood there, in the middle of the market bustle, eating chaat, at about 6.15 pm, he was pushed into a vehicle at gunpoint. His uncle, Md. Zaheer Alam who was on his way from Rai Bareilly to Allahabad, when informed of the abduction of his nephew rang up the SHO at Madiayun police station, who claimed to be away from the police station. The uncle sent faxes to the District Magistrate of Jaunpur, Chief Minister, the Governer as well as the Home Secretary. On 21 December, a news item in the local newspapers appeared, which quoted Zaheer Falahi saying that he suspected his nephew had been killed in a fake encounter.

But this could as well have been happening on another planet, for this is how the FIR lodged in Barabanki Kotwali records the arrest of Tariq:

> Today, on 22.12.2007, secret information was received from an informer that a suspicious character with links to a terrorist organization, bearing deadly weapons and explosives, will be arriving at the Barabanki railway station at 6.30 am… around 6.15 am two persons got off from a rickshaw outside the station and began to wait for someone. The informer from a distance pointed towards one of these two men holding a bag. Suddenly these two picked up their bags and started walking quickly from the railway station towards the main road. We introduced ourselves and asked them to stop. They tried to open their bags. Knowing full well that their bags were laden with explosives, the members of the team [names] risked their lives in fulfilling the call of duty and finally caught them after some struggle.[2]

Bravo.

However, confronted by mounting public pressure, the then Chief Minister Mayawati ordered a probe into the allegations surrounding the arrest of hakim Tariq and Khalid Mujahid. The inquiry panel headed by Judge RD

---

2 FIR No. 1891/07, P.S. Kotwali, Barabanki. Copy on record. Translation from the original Hindi mine.

Nimesh that began work in 2008 was given a time frame of six months. It took the Commission more than four years to conclude hearings and submit its findings. The delay was partly on account of the long disappearances of the public prosecutor, and partly because the ATS was reluctant to participate in the hearings. In 2011, in the course of the Commission's proceedings, Sajadur Rehman, one of the co-accused in the Lucknow blast case was discharged for absolute lack of evidence.

Having examined 92 affidavits, 47 submitted by the state and 25 by the defence, the Nimesh Commission affirmed the account of Qasmi and Mujahid that they had been abducted by the STF. It concluded that their involvement in any incident on the morning of 22 December was doubtful, and indeed directed that those officers and personnel who had framed, illegally detained and tortured the duo be identified and prosecuted.[3]

Less than an year after the Commission submitted its report, Khalid Mujahid died of "sudden medical complications" while returning to Lucknow prison, having made his appearance in the court in Barabanki. Mujahid had no history of illnesses.

Don't be surprised by the fact that ten alleged operatives arrested in a midnight raid in Gulmohar colony in Khandwa on 13 June 2011 were actually picked up (again that dreaded phrase) between 10 and 12 June by the police from their homes in Ganesh ganj and Indira Nagar, ostensibly for questioning. They were never returned home – the police dismissed the families' pleas to return the boys, even feigned ignorance about their whereabouts. At least two families, that of Khaleel and Amjad, moved applications in court that their sons had been detained by

---

3 Report of the One-Member Nimesh Inquiry Commission, submitted on 31 August 2012, copy on record.

the police without any charge and the police had failed to produce them before court within 24 hours as they are bound to.[4] In response to these applications, the City Kotwali police submitted to the Chief Judicial Magistrate that though Khaleel had been called to the police station on 10 June, he had not been detained thereafter. The police also claimed that Amjad had not been found at all despite their investigations and therefore could not be questioned. These responses are dated 13 June.[5] On 15 June however, news headlines announced that the local police had arrested 10 SIMI activists from Aquil Khilji's house in Gulmohar Colony. The police had busted a meeting on the night of 13 June when they were "reviewing their future actvities" and "planning a terror strike".[6] IG (ATS) Vipin Maheshwari told *Times of India* that the police recovered "four pistols, 12 live cartridges, SIMI literature, two dozen CDs and phones."[7] Only the most senseless and the foolhardiest would have convened a meeting days after being questioned by the police. The CJM before whom the accused were produced noted in his order granting the

---

4 Applications in the Court of the CJM, Khandwa, *Khaleel (s/o Ismail Chauhan) vs The State of Madhya Pradesh* through City Kotwali PS u/s 437 CrPC read with 56 CrPC (dated 12 June 2011 and *Amjad (s/o Ramzan) vs The State of Madhya Pradesh*, through Arakshi Kendra, City Kotwali, Khandwa u/s 437 CrpC (dated 10 June 2011). Copies on record.

5 Communication of the SHO, Kotwali P.S. to CJM. Copy on record.

6 "10 SIMI men held in MP raid" by Milind Ghatwai, *Indian Express*, 15 June 2011. http://archive.indianexpress.com/news/10-simi-men-held-in-mp-raid/803720/. Also see http://daily.bhaskar.com/article/MP-BHO-10-simi-activists-get-arrested-in-khandwa-madhya-pradesh-2190536.html

7 "MP ATS arrests 10 SIMI Men", *Times of India*, 15 June 2011. http://timesofindia.indiatimes.com/india/MP-ATS-arrests-10-SIMI-men/articleshow/8857605.cms

police remand that there were blue bruises on the body of Khaleel.[8]

* * *

It is interesting how counterterror agencies are drawn towards bus and railway stations, almost as moths to light. Most arrests are shown as taking place in and around bus stations and railway stations. Irshad and Qamar were shown alighting from a Kashmir Roadways bus at Mukarba Chowk, North Delhi – it turned out that the bus tickets placed as evidence before the court were of a day later than the purported date of arrest. In November 2009, Additional Sessions Judge Dharmesh Sharma noted that the Special Cell's story of having nabbed Gulzar Ahmed Ganai and Md. Amin Hajam – 'dreaded terrorists' of the LeT – at Mahipalpur Chowk at 9.15 pm when they were de-boarding bus number DLIPB 0249 (route number 729) fell flat in view of the testimonies of the bus conductor and owner that the said bus did not ply at all in the evening of 10 December 2006, the supposed date of the arrest.

Bus stations and rail stations are significant to most plots of the investigative agencies as they are the sites where the accused are trying to pass on "arms and explosives" to someone leaving town or arriving from out of town. So even while according to the police story, invariably, their secret informer, *mukhbir*, tells them of a rendezvous terrorists have fixed to pass on arms, explosives and such like to their aides, the police shows little keenness in apprehending the aides whom the terrorist was supposedly standing in wait for; or indeed in tracing the explosives and cash seized from the accused. Delighted at

8 Order of CJM DS Chauhan in Crime No. 319/11, dated 14 June 2011.

having nabbed a 'kingpin' and recovered suitable caches of money, detonators etc. – the investigators then get busy extolling their commitment to duty in press conferences. In some cases at least, courts have shown that money and arms were planted on the accused. The Special Cell alleged in the FIR that a search of the accused Gulzar Ganai and Md. Hajam yielded 15 slabs of oil-based explosives, Rupees six lakh in cash and two non-electric detonators. The police diary, however, when perused by Judge Sharma revealed no such information about the recoveries. This, and the contradicting testimonies about the recoveries in the court by the members of the Special Cell, drove the judge to wonder if it was a "human mistake or something else. The moot point is: were the mistakes pointed out above bonafide or mistakes committed while attempting to cook up the entire story?"

Similarly, the CBI too, while investigating the Qamar and Irshad Ali case, noted that the Special Cell remained unperturbed by the recoveries of explosives and cash, not deigning to track the arms trail. This suggested that these were no recoveries but plants. The question, then, is where are these recoveries procured from? Who is paying for the lakhs being shown as recovered, where does the trail of RDX and arms and ammunition lead to?

The Home Minister, speaking at the same programme alluded to above, complained that Indians' idea of counter terror ops, influenced by cinema, was of someone chopping off bomb wires with nervous, sweaty hands, just moments before the bomb is to explode. But it appears the Indian public aren't the only ones raised on a diet of Bollywood masala – the security establishment, too, is a firm believer in the value of theatre. Why else would they transform illegal detentions and abductions into dramatic arrests and heroic encounters with terrorists? One understands that there can be false leads and even faulty investigations – but to assert that a blast case has been solved, or a terror module busted on the basis of forced disclosures and custodial confessions is a lapse of another order.

So then how does one believe the Special Cell which has been proven to plant evidence on innocents – proven guilty not by civil rights groups, but by the CBI and courts – implicating them in false cases as operatives of Al Badar, LeT or agents of ISI, when it now says that the young men, one of them practically a boy, killed in the Batla House encounter were key figures in the IM hierarchy.

Activists and legal rights workers often advise those vulnerable to such arrests and illegal detentions that in the event someone is taken away unlawfully without identification or papers, a missing persons complaint should be lodged at the earliest. That copies should be sent to as many State institutions as possible to record the period of illegal detention. Within a couple of hours of Abu Bashar being taken away, his younger brother sent an email to the Supreme Court describing frantically how some men posing as guests came to their Beenapra home and took away Bashar. He said that he feared that the visitors belonged to the UP STF. Bashar's brother may have hoped that this email would be converted into a writ of habeas corpus. Instead, the supreme court of justice replied more than a month later through the Assistant Registrar of its PIL Cell that "no action can be taken on your petition as the subject matter of your Email does not cover [sic] under any of the guidelines prescribed to deal with PIL matters. You may, if so advised, approach the appropriate forum for the desired relief, as per law."[9]

Bashar's father not only reported his missing son to the police station, but he also wrote to the whole range of offices available in our democracy, including the National

9 Communication Dy No. 8011/SC PIL/2008 dated 17 September 2008.

Human Rights Commission. To the NHRC, he wrote not only of the unlawful taking away of his son, but also of the apathy of the local police and the abuse and violence by the ATS whilst it conducted a raid in his house. What did the NHRC do? Issue notice to the ATS? Seek a response from the Commissioner of Police? No, it simply redirected the complaint to the SSP, Azamgarh, asking the complaint to be disposed "at your end". End of matter.

And then there are inquiry commissions. Like the Nimesh Commission, which was tabled in the Uttar Pradesh Assembly only after the custodial death of Khalid Mujahid – and after mass uproar over his death.[10] As a rule, governments prefer not to table these reports, believing firmly in the credo that time heals all. This is precisely the fate of Advocate Ravi Chander Report examining the allegations of torture and forced confessions in the Mecca Masjid blasts and the Bhaskar Rao Commission looking into the police firing on those protesting the blast in the mosque. In 2010, responding to a question raised on the floor of the Andhra Pradesh Assembly, the incumbent Chief Minister Kiran Reddy insisted that he would apologize in the Assembly if the inquiry reports corroborate the accusations of torture.[11] Only he wouldn't table the reports so we know. There is another approach too – brazenly ignore all calls for impartial inquiry and hide behind an effete NHRC which submits its report on an encounter

---

10 "Nimesh Commission Report tabled at UP Assembly", *The Hindu*, 17 September 2013. http://www.thehindu.com/news/national/other-states/nimesh-commission-report-tabled-at-up-assembly/article5135058.ece

11 "Mecca Masjid: Govt ready to Apologise to Muslim Youth", *Indian Express*, 16 December 2010. http://archive.indianexpress.com/news/mecca-masjid-ap-govt-ready-to-apologise-to-muslim-youth/725644/

killing on the basis of police statements, which is what happened in the Batla House case.

If stories about 'home grown terror' are to be reported solely on the basis of confessions, disclosures, interrogation reports, and opinions of so-called security experts, then no doubt there will emerge the "picture of a shadowy, sinister outfit of brainwashed young men", about whom journalists can write simultaneously without a trace of irony that these youth are so socially integrated as to be indistinguishable from any other boys their age – as well as driven by "alienation from the Indian society". There is no precise count of how many are arrested, under trial or convicted in terror related cases. But we can be certain that the assertion glibly bandied around that this new breed of terror suspects are doctors, engineers, 'techies', college educated and professionals, does not correspond to reality. In Hyderabad, auto mechanics and drivers were picked up; in Uttar Pradesh, a mufti among others; poor daily wagers and construction workers have been arrested in Madhya Pradesh.

Even the so-called IT stories are really stories of struggle and often the first generation breaking into higher education and professions. Sarwar, son of a Mathematics teacher, known to all as Master Saab of Chandpatti (Azamgarh), was sent for IIT coaching to Benaras but when he could not clear JEE in two attempts, he joined Integral University in Lucknow. "He always stood first", his mother recalls as she caresses the file that holds his degrees and testimonials. Sarwar wanted to pursue M.Tech but they lacked the resources to fund his studies. "We were ready to sell the farm land", his father says, "but Sarwar wouldn't let me". Instead, he decided to work and enroll in M.Tech as a private student. "We were so happy when he got the job. We thought our days would change now." Sarwar's mother lets out a loud wail: "if only I had known, I wouldn't have let him out of my sight. We would have eaten meagrely, but would not have sent him to earn in another city."[12]

Piece together the story of Ranchi's Danish 'Reyaz' from the interrogation reports, which surfaced in major newspapers and you will see a cunning software engineer operating multiple emails, plotting and planning kidnappings for ransom and bank robberies to raise funds for a tattered IM organization.[13]

Like many of his generation, IT had seduced Danish too. Completing his BA (Hons.) in Geography, Danish enrolled at the Indian Institute of Hardware technology, one of those many private colleges that sell dreams of social mobility to young men like Danish. Financial constraints forced him to drop out of the last year of his course, sending him instead to Mumbai, that waiting post en route to Middle East. He lodged with an Urdu bookshop owner – also named Danish Reyaz – in Meera Road, in the time that he looked for employment in the Gulf. Without his certificate from the IT institute, he remained singularly unsuccessful. And in the manner of many fickle minded, unlucky and unemployed young men, had to return to Ranchi now to complete his course. He completed it in 2007. For a while repairing computers in Ranchi, Danish left for Hyderabad in 2008, in the hope of a white collar job, comforted by the presence of other young men from Baryatu, Ranchi's Muslim neighbourhood, who now lived and worked in the city. When the crime branch came to his family home in November-December 2008 (his brother could not recall the exact dates), he was already in Hyderabad, and dismissed the visit as a case of

12 Personal interview.

13 "Indian Mujahideen Strapped for Cash, Says Arrested Suspect", Rediff.com, 28 June 2011. http://www.rediff.com/news/column/im-on-the-backfoot-suspect-tells-gujarat-cops/20110628.htm

mistaken identity – perhaps a confusion of names. His landlord Danish Reyaz had been picked up briefly after the Mumbai train blasts by the ATS, but never charged.

Danish's name first surfaced publicly, along with that of his neighbour and friend Manzar Imam, in local newspapers in Ranchi on 15 December 2010. "Two among IM operatives hail from Baryatu" was the general tenor of headlines.[14] The same day, his brother saw his photograph being flashed on a news channel. Visits by media and the local crime branch were followed by a few months of peace. In April 2011, a team of NIA men visited Baryatu. "They were South Indian men who first posed as personnel of the passport office", recalled his brother who was home when the team arrived. They left the number of the DSP, NIA, in Hyderabad, asking for Danish to contact him.

The private correspondence between Danish and his brother 'R' from those days reveals another man altogether: a young, unsure and vulnerable Danish – hardly the crafty organizer of terror attacks that he was portrayed to be.[15]

> R: Is everything alright there?
> D: yes.
> R: Did you receive any more phone calls? The person who used to call you from Ranchi.
> D: No.
> R: Oh, that's a relief… Did anyone try to meet you?
> D: No.

---

14 "Yet another Attempt to Manufacture Muslim "Terrorists" by Mahtab Alam, Twocircles.net, 21 December 2010. http://twocircles.net/2010dec21/yet_another_attempt_manufacture_muslim_%E2%80%98terrorists%E2%80%99.html

15 Based on personal communication between Danish and his brother 'R' in the period 15 April to 25 April 2011. Copy on record.

R: You gave them your address. Maybe they are watching.
D: Perhaps they are busy in something else. I have told my office also. To my HR.
R: What did you say?
D: They have told me not to worry. They have promised me that they will help if there is any problem.
R: Inshaallah. But what did you tell them?
D: I have told them that perhaps there is a misconception because of the names.

R: Give our number to the office so that they can call in case of any emergency.
Danish: OK.
R: Yes, do it, if possible.
D: Inshaallah, there won't be an emergency.
R: We are all praying for that.
R: This problem won't be solved till you see him. In fact it will only increase.
R: Hello, where are you Danish?
D: He just called.
R: Who? The DSP?
D: Yes, from Hyderabad.
R: What did he ask?
D: He said he would call again at 11 tomorrow.
R: OK.
D: He was asking for the office and room address.
R: OK.
D: He was asking if I could meet him tomorrow.
R: You must tell him everything truthfully.
R: So what did you tell?
D: I told them that I had gone to Mumbai...
...

D: Then he took the details of both the offices I have worked in.
...

R: Why just two offices? What about the first one?
D: I don't have any proof of that. But I have given the address of that office also.
...

D: He had promised to pay me salary after 3 months.
D: He used to pay everyone by cheque
R: Did he ever give you any salary?
D: No...
D: He was asking me how my name came up. With father's name.
R: Good you explained to him everything.
D: I told him I stayed with Danish for three months, in connection to job searching.
...

D: He showed me a paper, where father's name was mentioned also.
R: OK.
D: I told him that about 4 months ago some people had come for investigation after my name first appeared in the papers. The neighbours must have given father's name to them.
R: Then?
D: Then he understood everything.
D: He only wanted to know where I was in December 2007.
R: OK. Then?
D: I told him I was in Ranchi and I have proof for that. He told me to leave then. He said come with your certificate when I call you.
R: OK.
D: Then he photographed me from 3-4 angles and recorded my voice
R: Then?
D: Then he told his assistant to take me out for tea-coffee.

This conversation, above all tells us two things: first, the belief of the brothers that telling the truth would protect them.

In the end though their faith proved to be misplaced. Barely two weeks after Danish visited the NIA office in Hyderabad to offer himself for questioning, he was shown arrested from the Vadodara railway station by Gujarat ATS for involvement in Gujarat blasts of 2008.

And second, it tells us how these imaginings of terror accused being cosmopolitan IT prodigals are quite hollow. Here is a young man who worked months without an appointment letter, without a salary slip – and without a salary – now worrying how the free labour extracted by an exploitative market has obliterated his legal existence, leaving him with no proof about his activities in those months. "But at least he [the former employer] can give witness that he employed you," asks the elder brother tentatively. But they both know the answer to that. It's unlikely.

It is an irony – surely an unintended one, that while these suspects are expected to recall their lives, as though in a flashback, with precise proof, no less, of every single day, the rest of the public which consumes the stories of their arrests is hoped to be in possession of very short memories.

In fact, that's what the Indian investigating agencies depend on. They live in the hope that their claims of busting terror modules will not be questioned – that their methods will be condoned and when the confessions they manufacture through torture of suspects militate against evidence and common sense, all will be forgotten. And so the next cycle will begin – on a clean slate, as if nothing happened. New suspects can always be rounded up – abducted even – and paraded sensationally as masterminds and operatives.

It falls on us then, to keep stoking the fire of memories – not for breast-beating, but to ensure the end of impunity.

Malegaon and the fiction of Muslim Revenge

> "On the day of *shab-e baraat*, Riyaz told me to finish my work early and reach the Bada Kabristan by noon. Riyaz, Rais and two others were already present when I reached ... They handed me one cycle... Then I saw the bomb that we had prepared the previous night, wrapped in a black bag tied to the carrier of the cycle. I parked the cycle in the parking lot of the madrasa opposite the masjid. Then I saw Riyaz hand Rais a black bag carrying a bomb. Rais hung the bag on the gate of the Kabristan. Riyaz and the two strangers who were with him then hung the bomb bag on the wall of the powerhouse opposite the wazukhana."

Thus was recorded Noorul Hooda's confession by the Superintendent of Police of Thane Rural on 22 November 2006. His confessional statement under Section 18 of MCOCA became one of the crucial pieces of 'evidence' in the ATS' investigation in the Malegaon bombings of September 2006.

The ATS chargesheet carried all the hallmarks of a classic terror investigation in our country: a set of accused with a SIMI past – seizures of 'jihadi' literature pretending to attest to that; secret meetings to discuss and carry out jihad. Training in arms and bomb making. A Pakistani connection turning it into an international conspiracy. And finally a voluminous chargesheet whose sheer size has the ability to crush and destroy the spirit of the accused.

Hefty chargesheets are often a key part of the psy-ops in the war on terror. The Malegaon chargesheet ran into over 2200 pages. But in brief, the prosecution case was as follows: a group of men – among them unani doctors, owners of battery shops, labourers, unemployed youth – had conspired to engineer communal riots by blasting bombs in the masjid on the holy day of *shab-e baraat*. Some of them had earlier received training in arms and bombs in Karachi, which they had reached via Dubai. When the blasts – 4 in all, which killed 32 and injured 312 – failed to bring out Muslims in riotous mobs onto the streets of Malegaon, this module decided to plant another bomb, a fake one, comprising sand and RDX, in a mixed locality, hoping that it would produce the desired results.

Now that the NIA's supplementary chargesheet has destroyed the ATS case piece by piece, one can only imagine the torture that must have driven an innocent man to incriminate himself and others accused in the blasts. The ATS is known to house an apparatus of indescribable cruelty – not the random, routine violence that our police thanas are known for – but hardcore nuts and bolts, clinical kind of torture involving noxious gases, stinging burning oils, even cockroaches – supplemented often by narco tests. Few can emerge from their chambers without signing a voluntary confessional.

The investigation was handed over to ATS on 23 October 2006, and as if by magic, the conspiracy unspooled itself, leading to a flurry of arrests, all accused gripped by a strong urge to confess to their culpability in the blasts.

Though the ATS chargesheet ran into an overwhelming two thousand plus pages, listing 445 witnesses – the ATS proved to be singularly unlucky, incompetent, or plain callous, take your pick, in its list of witnesses. The witness to the preparation of bombs, the ace in the ATS's arsenal, fled to Allahabad to file an affidavit in the *Diwani adalat* that the agency had forced him to sign on a false statement before a magistrate. Another witness was found making an appearance repeatedly in the ATS panchnamas – being witness to both, the recovery of clothes of the deceased and the recovery of the fake bomb. The problem, however, being that both recoveries were made at the same time. There was little by way of evidence to substantiate the claims of arms training in Pakistan. Absolutely nothing to corroborate the comings and goings of Pakistani terrorists.

On the contrary, the NIA found numerous witnesses testifying that one of the alleged bombers was leading Friday prayers in Yavatamal, 400 hundred kilometres away, on the day of the blasts.

Even though bombs were planted on cycles, a test identification parade to ascertain who had procured those bicycles was never conducted by the ATS. In fact, the investigation tended to ignore the four bombs that had exploded within minutes of each other – three in the masjid and the fourth in the busy Mashawrat Chowk – to focus on the one that did not, an imitation, a mixture of sand and RDX, dangling from a wall four days later. This fake bomb, goes the ATS lore, led them to the godown of battery seller Shabbir, where the soil samples showed up RDX traces. The 'witnesses' to the seizure of soil samples later recanted. Shabbir became Accused Number 2 in the Malegaon blast case.

It did not strike the ATS chief, the bosses in the Maharashtra police hierarchy, or the authorities that sanctioned the invocation of the dreaded MCOCA, that Shabbir Masiullah had in fact been arrested at least a month prior to the blasts by the CB CID in connection with an alleged conspiracy to bomb the Ganesh Visarjan festival. Or that two other accused, Noorul Hooda and Riyaz, had been called into questioning by the Azad Nagar police station precisely three days prior to the blasts. Another accused Mohd. Zahid had earlier been booked in two other cases of conspiracy. How could this circle of men, under watch, even detention in Shabbir's case, manage to conspire and execute an attack of this scale involving the use of RDX?

It was no more than slight inconvenience that Shabbir was in judicial custody at the time of blasts. But neither this, nor the lack of evidence proved to be deterrence for obtaining sanction for the draconian MCOCA legislation.

Two thousand pages of lies and subterfuge. Who built it up, falsehood by falsehood?

ACP Kisan Shengal, in charge of investigating the Malegaon blasts also served on the team investigating the Mumbai train bombings earlier in July that year. Shengal in fact sewed the two cases together, charging two of the Mumbai accused with supplying RDX left over from the train bombings for the Malegaon blast. He sniffed out RDX traces from Shabbir's godown, just as he had recovered RDX from the home of an accused in the train blast case. The momentous crashing of Shengal's case has the potential to wreck the prosecution in Mumbai train blasts too.

But the fallout of the Malegaon frame-ups goes beyond simply one or two cases. It's significance lies in throwing up, yet again, the pattern of terror investigations. The marking out of Muslim population as suspect and the breeding of informers, who themselves can be sacrificed without compunction – which Abrar Ahmed, accused number 9 was to discover – as the *sin qua non* of the relationship between police agencies and Muslims. Malegaon must also be held up as an example of how the constructed idea of Muslim rage and revenge has congealed our national narrative of terrorism. Every single confession – dictated now we know by the ATS – alluded to the 2002 Gujarat pogrom, the Malegaon riots that preceded it, and the thirty felled mosques that were calling out to be avenged.

Across the country the prosecution habitually submits videos of Gujarat violence, allegedly recovered from the accused, as proof that they had been 'radicalized' and prepared for jihad. Malegaon shows us how facile and constructed this narrative is.

Abrar Ahmed, the 33-year old electrician from Malegaon ostensibly dictated his confessional statement to Deputy Commissioner of Police, Zone I, Mumbai, soon after he was arrested by the Mumbai ATS. 'Revealing' details of the meeting of SIMI activists where the conspiracy of Malegaon blasts was hatched, he said:

> In this meeting, Dr. Salman, Dr. Farog, Munnawar and Shabbir told us how in 2001 our mosques had been razed and our Muslim brethren killed. We should avenge these at any cost... we were already burning with the desire for revenge – we only needed someone to show us the way. The police, administration and the Hindus had inflicted brutal repression on us. Dr. Salman and Dr. Farog lectured to us about that. Mohammad Zahid filled us with enthusiasm and energy by encouraging us to avenge this repression by exploding bombs in Malegaon, and if need be, to use arms as well.

Were the officers who recorded these false statements willing partners of ATS, or had the threat of more violence turned the accused into reluctant participants in the charade of voluntary confessions? It demonstrates how inherently dangerous it is to rely on laws like MCOCA which have at their core confessions recorded by policemen. But this is also precisely the usefulness of laws that admit confessions as evidence: lack of evidence substituted by torture confessions.

But most troublingly, it shows how easy it is to put away people for years. To charge them with crimes so heinous that they could possibly be sentenced to death. With no fear of consequences. Shameless prejudice is matched only by gross impunity. Whether Kisan Shengal will be tried for fabricating evidence and implicating innocents, or saved in the name of the ever-depleting morale of the investigators, we shall only know in some time.

Part II

Law of the Land

Death by Encounter

Early in the film, we see Nana Patekar walk into his house. He is laden with vegetables, bottle gourd, leafy coriander, the tools and symbols of homeliness. His wife is on the phone cooing instructions to someone about a sambhar recipe. Asafoetida (what is *qayam* in Hindi, she asks her husband, who mouths '*heeng*' to her) and ghee are the keys to a good sambhar she assures the person on the other side of the phone. And then she pushes her husband to the bathroom, pointing in the same good-natured way she was sharing her sambhar recipe, to the bloodstains on his white shirt. There is something exceedingly violent in this scene of domestic bliss. More violent than the ease with which Patekar has just been shown, moments ago, blowing the brains out of a gangster, his brag about his two mistresses in Kamathipura cut off in mid sentence.

The sweet domesticity doesn't contrast with the gritty violence of the highway. It is of a piece with it. This violence travels easily into the home. It has been normalized, naturalized, absorbed. It doesn't rankle, or prick. The rituals of daily life carried out with nonchalance immediately after the execution, reflect the acceptance of this kind of violence.

That was Patekar in *Ab Tak Chhappan* (56 and counting) reprising Pradeep Sharma's crime branch cop, whose killing count exceeded 105, at a time in his career when possibly his score was only on the half way mark.[1] There was a spate of films celebrating the exploits of the Mumbai 'encounter cops', some stylish and well crafted, but many simply crude. But were they manufacturing a public opinion in favour of vigilante justice or merely reflecting our society's condoning, if not overt approval of the phenomenon of extra judicial killing? The insularity of the Mumbai film industry may have led its filmmakers to recognize these killings and their film-worthiness only in the 1990s or later, when the streets of Mumbai, then Bombay, turned red with the blood of gangsters being felled equally by rival gangs and the crime branch. But as early as 1977, immediately after the Emergency, Jai Prakash Narayan constituted an inquiry committee headed by V.M. Tarkunde, to inquire into 77 cases of killings by police. Those killed were alleged to be Naxalites; these figures were drawn from the state of Andhra Pradesh alone – though killings were recognized to be widespread in Orissa and West Bengal as well – during the period of Emergency.

Read the Tarkunde Committee's report, *Encounters are Murders*, and cry. It could have been written today, the methods of elimination have hardly changed. The modus operandi of these killings was established early in the life our Republic. In its interim report released a month after it was founded, the Committee released facts about three encounters it had managed to investigate thus far.

---

1 *Ab Tak Chhappan* 2004, Director: Shimit Amin; Producer: Ram Gopal Verma.

Two of these – said to have occurred in Giraipally forest and Chilakalagutta forest – in which a total of eight people were killed, "never took place", the Committee concluded. There were witnesses who saw them being taken away by the police from their homes; witnesses who saw them being tortured brutally in police custody; witnesses, in the second encounter case, who saw them being driven away in a police vehicle covered with tarpaulin, while the men inside screamed and pleaded that they were being taken away to be killed; and finally, in the first encounter, even a witness, who saw them being shot in cold blood by the police, less than 50 feet away, as he stood hidden in the darkness of the Giraipally forest.

There was ample circumstantial evidence to "cast serious doubts on the official reports" about the third encounter of two "unidentified Naxalites" – one of whom was later identified as Neelam Ramachandriah, an ex-MLC. Ramachandriah, it was confirmed by witnesses, had been present in Vijaywada the night before the encounter allegedly took place in Yulladu forests, eighty kilometers away, with no direct bus link.[2]

But again, just as our methods of killing were perfected early, so were the means to thwart justice. The explosive findings of the Tarkunde Committee forced the Janata government to form the Justice Bhargava Commission. Indeed, the Tarkunde Committee had emphasized political patronage and government complicity in the encounters and demanded the institution of an independent commission of inquiry. However, any possibilities for justice were foreclosed by the Commission's narrow terms of reference, excluding from its purview the apportioning of responsibility for the murders. But even when assured

---

2 "'Encounters' are Murders: Interim Report of the Civil Rights Committee", *Economic and Political Weekly*, Vol. 12, No. 21, 21 May 1977, pp. 827-829.

of protection from prosecution, the state government declined to submit official documents, in many cases destroying them. Witnesses who deposed before the Commission were hounded and threatened, and finally, when a witness, K Lalitha testified that no less than the IG of the state had personally supervised her torture, the state practically disallowed the Commission to function. Somewhere perhaps the report of the Commission exists, but it was never published though officially submitted. None of those who carried out the killings in the Garaipally forests were ever punished.[3]

K Balagopal's reports from the ground through the 1980s indicate that the lifting of Emergency had little impact on killings by the police. If anything, the scale and severity only increased. Where Vengal Rao, home minister during the Congress regime, had preened about his government 'wiping out Naxalites', Vasant Nageswar Rao, home minister in the NTR government, described encounters as "routine affair". A police force reared on a robust diet of impunity to torture and kill was now being fattened with cash rewards. Even if we dismiss the rumour of Rs 20,000 for each head as mere hearsay, the Home Minister did hold public meetings to disburse cash rewards to policemen involved in encounter killings.[4]

With KPS Gill's arrival in Punjab, the headhunting and bounty system was formalized. Allegations swirled that letters were dispatched to all district senior superintendents sanctioning rewards in exchange for arrest or liq-

---

3 *Police Killings and Rural Violence in Andhra Pradesh*, Human Rights Watch, 1992, pp. 9-10.

4 *Encounter Killings in Andhra Pradesh, Excerpts from Reports of AP Civil Liberties Committee*, Hyderabad, 1985. Available at: http://www.unipune.ac.in/snc/cssh/HumanRights/02%20STATE%20AND%20ARMY%20-%20POLICE%20REPRESSION/A-%20Andhra%20pradesh/10.pdf

uidation of "wanted extremists/terrorists". A list with 53 names and addresses was appended with the instructions.[5] Earlier this year in 2013, a sub inspector Surjit Singh announced before the media that he had killed 83 Sikh youth in fake encounters in the 1990s at the prompting of his seniors, in particular naming SSP Paramjit Singh Gill. "I was a constable (sipahi) and I was promoted as SHO. What was the reason for it? – that I and Gill Sahib both know", reflecting the institutionalisation of the incentive to kill.[6]

Such was KPS Gill's power, and so beyond reproach and question was his encounter policy that Governor Virender Verma was transferred to another state when he declared his intention to end the reign of false encounters. Gill accused Verma of demoralizing the police force when his advisor as well as the Home Secretary recommended action against police officers involved in the torture and subsequent execution – passed off predictably as a killing in self defence – of two students Harpal Singh and Baljit Singh in June 1990.[7]

It must be remembered that in March 1988 both houses of the Parliament passed the 59th amendment, which suspended all rights including the right to life in the state of Punjab. For close to five years, the right to life did not exist in this state, with the approval of the Parliament.

5 Report of the UN Special Rapporteur on Extrajudicial, Summary or Arbitrary Executions, 1990, para 211, p. 54.

6 http://www.sikhsiyasat.net/2013/07/02/i-killed-83-innocent-sikhs-in-staged-encounters-on-directions-of-high-ups-in-punjab-police-surjit-singh-si/

7 *Human Rights Violations in Punjab: Use and Abuse of the Law*, Amnesty International, May 1991. Available at: *http://www.amnesty.org/en/library/asset/ASA20/011/1991/ru/d0c5a939-f944-11dd-92e7-c59f81373cf2/asa200111991ar.html*; See also *Dead Silence: The Legacy of Human Rights Abuses in Punjab*, HRW and Physicians for Human Rights, 1994, p. 13.

However, as has been said, the suspension of the right to life did not automatically confer upon the police forces the right to kill.[8] But this is precisely what happened. Dogged and courageous campaigners went about documenting these abuses at great personal peril – in many cases it proved fatal, as they were eliminated by those whose excesses they were recording. Jaswant Singh Khalra calculated the number of dead and the disappeared from the amount of wood consumed by various crematoria; there were numerous reports carrying the testimonies of families who had witnessed their sons being taken away – the lucky ones were returned the bodies of their sons; countless others just disappeared, ending either in the crematoria or dumped in the numerous canals and waterways of Punjab. In many of these documents, police officers or the dreaded men of Criminal Investigation Agency (CIA) are named, registration numbers of vehicles which ferried away men from their homes and fields are provided – on the occasion that the vehicles bore number plates, police stations where they were taken are recounted. Iqbal Singh for instance recounted to Ram Narayan Kumar – one of the foremost chroniclers of this period – in detail about his torment at the hands of CIA staff at Ladha Kothi, an interrogation centre, later converted into a jail. He could recognize the officers who abducted him, those who supervised his humiliation and torture; as well as the men who were taken out each night to be killed in fake encounters.[9]

Despite the meticulous documentation by Sikh and human rights groups of utter contempt of the Punjab police for rule of law, and despite the termination of virtual

---

8 Anil Nauriya, "Hiss of the Serpent", *Economic and Political Weekly*, Vol. 23, No. 24, 1988, pp. 1211-1214.

9 *State Terrorism in Punjab: A Report* by Committee for Information and Initiative on Punjab, New Delhi 1989.

emergency, accountability has been near nil. Successive governments, even those headed by Akali Dal, whose own members had borne the brunt of the police rule, continued to protect those responsible for the killing, maiming, torture and disappearance of thousands in the state.

The State's Strategies

Nearly 67 years after independence, we are still struggling for this minimum: that after every killing arising from police action, the police be required to prove that they killed in self defense. Article 21, the right to life, should have been an automatic guarantor of this. We have seen, however, that the State is far too reluctant to grant the citizens this right, affording itself and its agencies a position above law. The response of the State has been along three interrelated lines – and it has remained stunningly committed to this line of argument. Its first strategy is to unleash a barrage of such breathtakingly sterile language that it overwhelms you with its officialese – a leaden bureaucratic deflection of issues.

Between 1982, when the UN passed a resolution to appoint a special rapporteur to examine the occurrence and extent of the practice of extrajudicial, summary or arbitrary executions, and 2011, when India finally extended a standing invitation to the mandate-holders of all thematic special procedures of the Human Rights Council, the UN Special Rapporteur made do with communications with the Government of India. Year after year, the special rapporteurs would record in their annual reports India's reluctance, silence in fact, on their wish to visit India to examine the allegations of encounters and executions, and lament its non cooperation with the UN's mandate. Official communications were raised to an art of obfuscation.

In August 1992, the UN Special Rapporteur wrote to the Government of India about 95 cases of alleged extrajudicial, summary or arbitrary executions – in two of these, the victims were said to be minors.[10]

A few months later, the GOI responded, not with any details about the 95 cases, but with the happy news of the decision taken at a chief ministers' conference to set up a national human rights commission. The purpose of the Commission, claimed the missive, was "to instill a sense of confidence in the Indian people regarding the commitment of the Government and society at large to the cause of human rights." "Any human rights violations anywhere in India should be dealt with sternly", the CMs' conference piously resolved.[11]

In a subsequent 'communication', the Special Rapporteur was informed that "even in States so affected by terrorism and insurgency as Jammu and Kashmir, to which most of the allegations related, the law enforcement officials performed their obligations in accordance with the Code of Conduct for Law Enforcement Officials. Every allegation of human rights violations was scrupulously investigated and most of them were found inaccurate, highly exaggerated or deliberately false."[12]

Obviously then, in such an idyllic world – a veritable haven of human rights – a body such as the NHRC could play only a limited role.

Dead, Hence Guilty

A complaint by the APCLC drawing the NHRC's attention to 295 cases of encounter killings resulted in the issuance of its guidelines in 1997. At the heart of the procedure laid out was the simple rule that prima facie a death

---

10 Para 335, Available at: http://www.ensaaf.org/publications/other/Rapporteur_on_executions_1993.pdf

11 ibid., para 340.

12 ibid., para 347.

arising from police firing satisfied the ingredients of culpable homicide, necessitating registration of information and investigation. However, as the Chairperson of the NHRC wrote in his letter to the chief ministers: "under the scheme of criminal law prevailing in India, it would not be an offence if the death is caused in exercise of right of private defence. Another provision under which the police officer can justify causing the death of a person, is Section 46 of the Criminal Procedure Code."

Indeed, Section 46 of the Criminal Procedure Code is the trigger for the State's second strategy: that is to produce a narrative of guilt of those killed in encounters. This Section grants police the powers to use all means necessary to effect an arrest if the suspect uses force or attempts to evade arrest. But it also warns that "Nothing in this Section gives a right to cause the death of a person who is not accused of an offence punishable with death or with imprisonment for life." While it may have been intended originally to dissuade police from applying force indiscriminately, it has had the effect of presenting us with a strange paradox. A is killed; A is alleged to be guilty of crimes attracting death or life sentence; thus A has been killed in good faith; ergo the encounter is genuine. If the genuineness of an encounter killing is to be built on the guilt of the encountered, there is an immediate shift in discourse. The police only need demonstrate an allegation to justify an encounter, shifting the burden of proving their innocence on those killed. And as is well known, dead people don't talk. This is the ultimate convenience of encounter killing.

In the 1990s, when the body count was spiraling in Mumbai, two civil rights groups, the Committee for the Protection of Democratic Rights (CPDR) and the People's Union of Civil Liberties (PUCL), were moved to petition the High Court seeking an inquiry into two encounter killings in 1997: the killing of Javed Fawda alias Abu Sayama and Sada Pawle and Vijay Tandel, also said to be criminals. The Samajwadi Party also filed a petition asking for an inquiry into the killing of a criminal Javed Fawda.

Taking up the three petitions jointly, the High Court ordered an inquiry into the two encounters.[13] The inquiry carried out by Judge AS Aguiar, principal judge of the Bombay Sessions Court, was held in February-March 1998 and submitted to the High Court in July of the same year. He declared both encounters to be fake. The High Court however did not accept the Commission's conclusions and held both encounters to be genuine. But what was significant was that Judge Aguiar's report carried a section titled, "Trigger Happy Cop" which detailed the past of API Dhobale, the policeman who had admitted to having fired at Javed Fawda. The Commission's report recalled that Assistant Police Inspector Dhobale had been convicted for the custodial death of one Abdul Gaffar Khan by the trial court in 1994. (The High Court had set the conviction aside and a SLP was pending in the Supreme Court).

Judge Aguiar noted, with a scarcely veiled disapproval, that during cross examination, API Dhobale could not even recollect the number of people he had killed in encounters: "encounter-killing it appears, is no big deal. It had become a routine affair."[14]

The High Court, however, was none too pleased with the allusion to API Dhobale's past record, saying it had

13 *PUCL vs the State of Maharashtra and Others*, Bombay High Court, Author A.P.Shah; Bench: AP Shah and J Patil, 10 December 1997. Available at http://indiankanoon.org/doc/807655/

14 *The Aguiar Commission Report on the Extra Judicial Executions by the Bombay Police*, 15 July 1998, p. 20. Accessed at: http://www.oocities.org/indianfascism/fascism/bombay1.htm

"nothing to do with the legal exercise expected to be done by the learned Inquiry Judge." On the contrary, it places great emphasis on the sworn affidavit of the Commissioner of Police and another police officer detailing the cases registered against the deceased Sada Pawle and Vijay Tandel in various police stations: "From this, it can be deduced without any hesitation that the said two deceased are the dreaded gangsters and if not notorious criminals, always indulged in committing serious offence in the Mumbai Metropolis."[15] (sic)

Is it any surprise that the breathless commentary and the deluge of leaked 'news' surrounding the CBI's investigation into the Ishrat Jahan encounter relentlessly focused on establishing her (non-existent) Lashkar links, as though somehow that would make the cold-blooded killing of this teenager palatable, or even justified. One single piece of paper of doubtful veracity, was frenziedly hyped as a 'New' story, a 'New' document to show the "slain Mumbai resident Ishrat Jehan Raza may have been an Lashkar-e Taiba terrorist." The documents referred to here were, of course, the much-flogged paragraphs from the Interrogation Report (IR) of David Headley referring to a botched up 'Ishrat module'. Much ink was spewed on the alleged excision of these 'tell-tale' paragraphs from the NIA's Interrogation Report of David Headley, available in the public domain[16] even while accepting that "The NIA note has little relevance to the murder investigation".[17]

---

15 *PUCL versus the State of Maharashtra and others*, Bombay High Court, Equivalent citations: 1999 (4) Bom CR 608; Author: N Arumugham Bench: N Arumugham, S R Desai.

16 Full text of the Interrogation Report here: http://www.investigativeproject.org/documents/case_docs/1602.pdf

17 "NIA note claimed Ishrat was with LeT" by Abhinandan Mishra, 22 June 2013, *Sunday Guardian*. Accessed at http://www.sunday-guardian.com/news/nia-note-claimed-ishrat-was-with-let; "Leaked NIA document indicates Cover up in Ishrat Jahan Case"

Unverified tapes of doubtful origin – alleged telephone conversations between a top Lashkar operative and his accomplices plotting the assassination of Narendra Modi – were played out on prime time as "The Ishrat Jahan Terror Tapes", even though Ishrat was not once named in the conversation.[18]

One journalist – known to be close to the BJP, though prone to seeking shelter in his professional identity whenever it got uncomfortable – said in a TV debate that regardless of which way the trial goes, once it is established in public perception that Ishrat Jahan was a terrorist, the BJP's then 'PM in waiting' could encash a political lottery out of it.

And once we have moved to this nebulous domain of guilt of the one who has died – and is no longer 'representable' in a court of law – the requirement that the agents of violence prove that they killed in self defense also withers away. Police's exercise of self defence becomes manifest, as though by itself.

The Lt. Governor of Delhi, in refusing to grant sanction for a magisterial inquiry in the Batla House encounter case said this:

> [W]hen the police went to apprehend the accused and they were fired upon, there was no option with them but to open fire in self defence and to arrest the accused. The modules of the Indian Mujahideen have conducted bomb explosions in various parts of the country including Delhi, Uttar Pradesh, Rajasthan, Gujarat, Karnataka, Andhra Pradesh etc. subjecting police officers, who have worked out this case at the cost

---

by Praveen Swami, 16 July 2013, *Firstpost*. Accessed at: http://www.firstpost.com/india/leaked-nia-document-indicates-cover-up-in-ishrat-jahan-case-958401.html

18 "Modi, Advani were in Ishrat Jahan's Hitlist", 14 June 2013, Centrestage, Headlines Today. Accessed at: http://headlinestoday.intoday.in/programme/ishrat-jahan-fake-encounter-case-narendra-modi-lk-advani-david-headley/1/280007.html

> of loosing [sic] a gallant colleague and nearly loosing [sic] another would be highly demoralizing and would weaken the resolve of the police officers to fight against terrorists. A police officer confronted by armed terrorists should not have to start thinking whether to die of the firing from the militants or if the militant dies to face the magisterial enquiries which are to follow. The Crime Branch is already conducting investigation of the shootout. Two accused persons are yet to be arrested. Crime Branch is expected to file its charge sheet in the Court shortly where after the case will be subjected to due judicial scrutiny. [19]

The Lt. Governor returns us to the tautological reasoning of guilt and murder. He deems it fit to not only pronounce his verdict in the Batla House encounter case – without an inquiry – but clearly settles it in favour of all police officers who must not be allowed to be 'demoralized' by magisterial enquiries which are to follow their 'fight against terrorists'. It also cleverly creates another fiction: that the crime branch is investigating the shootout. What the crime branch was investigating was the murder of Inspector Sharma. The deaths of Atif and Sajid having become inseparable from their alleged guilt – of being terrorists of Indian Mujahideen – apparently needed no resolution. In July this year, the sessions court convicted Shahzad Ahmed for the murder of Inspector Sharma despite the prosecution being unable to establish even his presence at the site of the encounter on that day.[20]

---

19 Communication received by the NHRC from the office of Deputy Secretary, Home, Cited in "NHRC Proceedings on the Batla House Encounter", 20 July 2009, pp. 11-12. Available at: http://nhrc.nic.in/batla.htm.

20 See *Beyond Reasonable Doubt? The Conviction of Shahzad Ahmed*, Jamia Teachers' Solidarity Association, August 2013. Available at http://document.teacherssolidarity.org/Beyond_Reasonable_Doubt-The_Conviction_of_Shahzad_Ahmad%20%E2%80%94_A_JTSA_Report.pdf.

Judge Shastri's order of sentencing gives us an unintended insight into what was playing on the court's mind while passing the verdict:

> Masses from entire Delhi were seen weeping and mourning the death of that brave heart (Inspector M.C. Sharma). Traumatized intellectuals from all over the country went in pensive mood. All this is evident as how said incident shocked collective conscience of the entire nation. This is also an aggravating factor against the convict.[21]

It was not law.

Law and Order

The corollary of this collective conscience, rather appropriately, is the vision of order that the State produces. Order, which is fragile and ever in danger of cracking and collapsing. Order, which can be held together by repression alone – agents of which must be protected from rule of law.

Between 1999 and 2008, a clutch of writ petitions pertaining to encounter killings in Andhra Pradesh were filed under Article 226 of the Constitution of India in the High Court.[22] A five-judge bench of the Andhra Pradesh High Court, combining these writs framed the following questions for consideration:

> 1. Where a police officer causes the death of a person, acting or purporting to act in discharge of official duties or in self-defence as the case may be, is there commission of a cognizable offence (including in an appropriate case the offence of culpable homicide); and whether the information relating to such circumstances requires to be registered as a First Information Report obligating investigation in accord-

---

21 *State versus Shahzad Ahmed @Pappu (*SC No. 42/10); Order on sentencing passed on 30 July 2013. Copy on record.

22 Writ Petition Nos.: 15419 of 2006; 26358 of 1999; 7906 of 2000; 14475 of 2002; 440 of 2003 and 857 of 2008.

ance with the procedure prescribed by the Code of Criminal Procedure, 1973?

2. Whether the existence of circumstances bringing a case within any of the exceptions in the Indian Penal Code, 1860 including exercise of the right of private defence could be conclusively determined during investigation; whether the final report submitted by the police officer to the Magistrate on completion of the investigation is conclusive or whether the existence of the circumstances coming within the exceptions requires to be determined only in appropriate judicial proceedings?

3. Whether a magisterial inquiry (whether under the Code of Criminal Procedure or extant Police Standing Orders) into the cause and circumstances of death occasioned by an act of a police officer obviate the rigor of investigation and trial of such act?

4. Whether the State, the police establishment or a police officer is immune from an obligation to disclose the identity of a Police Officer who had committed an act causing the death of a person, to enable an investigating officer or any person aggrieved by such death to effectively seek justice; and if so, in what circumstances or contexts?[23]

A counter affidavit filed in the Andhra Pradesh High Court by the Director General of Police of the state – in response to a petition filed by APCLC seeking the registration of crime in the offence of "killing of 8 Naxalites" in an encounter in the Nallamala forest on 23 July 2006 – invoked the spectre of a "red corridor from Nepal to Trivandrum right across the country, posing a threat to National Integrity" (in capitals in the original). "Remote devices", "exploding landmines", "sensational cases",

---

23 *Andhra Pradesh Civil Liberties Committee versus the Government of Andhra Pradesh*, In the High Court of Judicature of Andhra Pradesh at Hyderabad (Special Original Jurisdiction), 6 February 2009. Copy on record.

"creation of terror", "capture of power" summon a horrifying, fast unraveling dystopia.[24]

The Bench's judgement was a voluminous 50,000-word long, profound reading of substantive law, a meditation on Article 21 and a masterly survey of case law. The Bench's observations in response to killing by police officers was:

> On a careful consideration of the relevant statutory provisions; the binding and persuasive precedents; the normative architecture of private defense justifications generally and in the context of the provisions of the IPC; and the constitutional values that inform and structure our governance processes, we hold that the information conveyed to the officer in charge of a Police Station intimating the death of any person as a consequence of firing by law enforcement officials of the State (notwithstanding a claim as to the death occurring while exercising the right of private defence) must invariably and without exception be registered as FIR u/Sec. 154(1) Cr.P.C.; and investigation u/Sections 156/157 must follow.

The AP High Court's ruling would have impeded the routine of encounter killings and created a legal precedent which would have eroded the very basis of police impunity. Within days, therefore, the Andhra Pradesh Police Officers Association rushed to the Supreme Court for a stay. The Union of India surpassed the DGP's counter affidavit with its own apocalyptic tones in its affidavit in the SC: registration of criminal cases would threaten "the very existence of India as a nation state", "emasculate the functioning of security forces", and "gun wielding non State actors" would "hold the State and society to ransom".

---

24 In the High Court of Judicature of Andhra Pradesh at Hyderabad; WP No. 15419/2006, Counter affidavit filed by Swaranjit Sen, DGP, Andhra Pradesh, copy on record.

The AP High Court in directing that all cases of encounter killings be registered as cases of culpable homicide had utterly failed to recognize, in the Union of India's view, the contract between the individual and the State that underpins a "modern liberal democratic Nation": "In terms of this contract, an individual relinquishes some of the rights of his pre-State existence in return for security of life and property guaranteed by the state. The State enforces this covenant by raising the army, the paramilitary forces and the police..."[25]

How pitiful that the Indian State believes itself to be no more than a protection mafia. But it's worse. Theoretically at least, the Mafioso, even the most powerful ones, could be brought to justice. The Indian State is arguing instead "none of the legal principles of the Constitution ...are applicable under this since the security forces are not acting in their private capacities, but at the behest of the state."

This, then, is the third strategy. Of enveloping it's agents in a mantle of sovereignty and immunity.

But what would heroes be without formidable villains? What about Kasab, asks the Union of India. Should we have allowed Kasab the right to get a criminal case registered against the police/NSG officers? Kasab immediately invokes the apparition of a biryani chomping, jihad-crazed terrorist undeserving of the refinements of legal procedure, and becomes indeed a shorthand for all terror accused. A former judge of the Supreme Court, Justice Arijit Parsayat, speaking at a seminar at Indian Law Institute in Delhi on the theme of 'Investigation and

---

25 In the Supreme Court of India, 18910-15 of 2009 with 5933 of 2009; In the Matter of *Govt. of Andhra Pradesh and others [Petitioners] versus Andhra Pradesh Civil Liberties Committee and Others [Respondents]*; Counter affidavit filed by Union of India, Petitioner No. 2, copy on record.

Prosecution of Offences relating to Terrorism', described Ajmal Kasab as "not fit to be called a human. He is an animal." Naturally, therefore, the discourse of human rights does not apply to Kasab and other animals. ("So what is required is animal rights, not human rights," said the good judge).[26] And naturally, therefore, too, all those who argue for the rule of law, overlooking the simple dictum that human rights may not apply to a category of people are in grave error. These are the 'human rights alarmists' – credit must go to *Economic Times* for coining this term. In their affidavits and replies to the courts; in the public discussions, in the media and even films, human rights activists are the objects of ridicule, derision, and pure hatred – the perfect antithesis of the policemen and the security agencies, which put their life in danger to secure the country. From KPS Gill's letter to the Prime Minister heaping scorn on the "utterly compromised human rights lobby" whose campaign against extra judicial killings had driven Gill's trusted lieutenant in Tarn Taran, SSP Ajit Singh Sandhu to suicide, in 1997, to the Police Officers Association accusation that the petitioner APCLC "directly aids and abets the unlawful activities of the underground CPI (Maoist)", to the Union of India's counter-affidavit complaining that NGOs especially persuing (sic) human rights are adept at using the legal processes of the Indian State to …further the cause of the 'revolution'", human rights campaigners are set up as villains and their concerns malicious and worthy only of outright dismissal.

---

26 "Human Rights? Terrorists are animals, we need animal rights" by Tannu Sharma, 28 January 2009, *Indian Express*. http://www.indianexpress.com/news/human-rights--terrorists-are-animals-we-need-animal-rights/416004/

Checks and Balances

There is, it is argued, an established elaborate mechanism, which sifts and sieves the evidence, through whose fine mesh no fake encounter could possibly slip by.

The first of these alleged filters is the Investigating Officer. Sure, the IO could be expected to look at the evidence to judge if his colleagues had indulged in cold-blooded murder and include this in the chargesheet. Certainly, this rare manuscript must be hunted down and preserved for all. FIRs of encounter killings usually follow a template: where the deceased are booked under Section 307 of IPC along with related sections such as Arms Act, and the version provided by the police party involved in the encounter deaths is recorded as the 'facts of the case'. "The process of judicial oversight operates only after IO files the final report," claims the AP Police Officers Association. But the manner in which the IO records, investigates and then prepares the chargesheet, it is highly unlikely that the police are ever going to be subjected to judicial scrutiny.[27]

A reply from the office of the Delhi Police Special Cell in response to a RTI seeking details of encounter killings and officers involved was this: "The requisite information/list is enclosed herewith except the name of the police personnel and officials who encountered the accused persons which is exempted under Section 8 (1) (g) of RTI Act of 2005."

---

27 Just as the book was going to press, the Supreme Court in the matter of *PUCL & Anr versus State of Maharshtra* (Criminal appeals no. 1256 & 1367 of 1999, WP (C) No 316 of 2008, Contempt petition (C) No. 47 of 2011) laid down the procedure to be followed in the event of an encounter killing. Widely anticipated by the civil society, it too fell short of unambigiously directing the filing of FIRs against policemen involved in encounter killings.

Deceased equals accused in the police lexicon and procedure.

Even the FIR (448/97) first filed in the March 1997 killing of two businessmen, known famously as the Connaught Place fake encounter was registered "on the complaint of the then Inspector Anil Kumar of ISC Unit of Crime Branch". Inspector Anil Kumar was a member of the police party led by ACP SS Rathi, which shot dead Pradeep Goyal and Jagjit Singh. It was only when the family members of the dead men broke up the press conference being held by the Delhi Police to preen about the elimination of dreaded gangsters that mass outcry and bad publicity led to a CBI probe and subsequent conviction of Rathi, Anil Kumar and their juniors. The RTI reply from the Public Information Officer, Crime, New Delhi notes: "In this regard it is pertinent to mention here that initially the case was registered for encounter but later on as per the direction of the Hon'ble Court the case was converted into murder after conviction."[28] No departmental inquiry was ever held.

To say that the police can be relied upon to ensure that fake encounters will be punished is a myth that few will believe.

The second is the magisterial inquiry, a requirement in the NHRC's procedure. In a RTI application seeking details about the number of magisterial enquiries conducted in cases of encounter killings in Delhi, it emerged – in about six months' time and a great deal of correspondence later – that between 1995 and 2012, a grand total of two cases of deaths in encounters had been examined by magistrates.

In one case, known as the "Sonia Vihar encounter", I was told 'unofficially' that the magisterial inquiry report

---

28 Correspondence dated 22/05/2012. Copy on record.

was too explosive to be shared publicly. "Explosive as in damning?" Silent smiles. The 'official' line to deny me a copy of the report was that it would put to risk those who had deposed in the inquiry. Expose them to risk from whom? Those they had deposed against – the Special Cell officers? The replies from the NHRC were more illustrative. When asked for a copy of the magisterial report and all other documents pertaining to the case – the inquiry had been recommended by the NHRC following a complaint by the widow of the slain 'gangster' – I was sent the proceedings of the meetings held by the NHRC. In the meeting held on 19 April 2012, the inquiry officer (Principal Secretary Revenue) complained of the non cooperation of the police which was delaying the completion of the inquiry; in the 26 September meeting, his report, which recommended a CBI inquiry, was examined and the consent of the Government of NCT of Delhi sought to initiate the inquiry; on 20 December, the Commission notes with regret the extension of time sought by the Government of NCT of Delhi. But the proceedings of 6 March 2013 are silent on whether the permission for the CBI inquiry has been finally granted. It merely records that "The Investigation Division to analyze the MER submitted by the Divisional Commissioner, Revenue Department, Government of NCT of Delhi and submit a report within six weeks."

The key accused in the "Sonia Vihar encounter" case is ACP Sanjeev Yadav, a decorated and feted officer of the Special Cell, and the protagonist of many a FIR in encounter killings in Delhi.

In March 2014, the NHRC asked the Centre to pay compensation to the family of those killed in the encounter, calling it "doubtful". It also noted that the Delhi Police continued to stubbornly ignore the NHRC guidelines for holding magisterial enquiries. This stricture has however resulted neither in the stripping of these officers of their gallantry awards nor in any punitive action.[29]

As to the magisterial inquiry in the Swarn Jayanti Park encounter, there seemed to be no department willing to claim its possession, as the RTI application tortuously wound its way from the various sections of the Home Department to the SDM of the North West District of Delhi.[30]

The NHRC, touted as the third pillar of this edifice of 'checks and balances', has fancied itself as a compensation disbursing body rather than ensuring prosecution of police officers.

When the Supreme Court in 1996 appointed the NHRC to examine the Punjab mass cremations, it bestowed on it its extraordinary powers to conduct thorough investigation, fix accountability as well as reparations, under Article 32 of the Constitution. But the NHRC quickly grew nervous of this wide and sweeping mandate – possibly after SSP Sandhu's suicide and the subsequent fusillade launched by KPS Gill – and ignoring the SC's direction to consider "all the issues which are raised before the Commission by the learned counsel for the parties" refused to allow the families of the victims to depose, relying only on the police to identify the dead, and narrowing the inquiry to the crematoria in Amritsar.[31] This was an intimation of what the NHRC's chosen role would be in the coming years. In the Batla House encounter, it stood by as its own guidelines were flouted; and then finally prepared a polite report giving the Special Cell a clean chit based

29 http://www.deccanherald.com/content/390575/centre-asked-pay-doubtful-encounter.html

30 I finally received a copy of the report in February 2014, many months after I had applied for it.

31 *Protecting the Killers: A Policy of Impunity in Punjab*. 2007. Human Rights Watch. Available at: http://www.hrw.org/reports/2007/india1007/5.htm

on the statements of the senior police officers of the Delhi Police.

In 2012, when the Special Rapporteur on extrajudicial killings came calling on the NHRC he was informed that though the NHRC did receive "some complaints", the numbers did "not reflect a widespread practice or pattern in a country the size of India".[32]

In its catalogue of deaths that resulted from encounters with police and security agencies, NHRC included "individuals with criminal backgrounds" in Uttar Pradesh, "Naxals" in "the case of states affected by Naxalism" and "[I]n the Northeast, it is rare that someone completely innocent is killed by security forces."[33] This then is the list of encounterables of the Indian state.

You could be forgiven for mistaking the NHRC's lament that "while NGOs make allegations, often exaggerated, about the death of civilians in police action, they seldom talk about the death of police personnel" for a Home Ministry affidavit.[34] And why shouldn't you? The NHRC's rejection of the Optional Protocol of the ICCPR, requiring the creation of a body to hear individual complaints, was a barefaced reiteration of the official Indian position.[35] Even more brazen was its certification of the draconian Armed Forces Special Powers Act (AFSPA) as a just law: "very rarely has the Commission found that the AFSPA is itself the problem; most times the problem

32 Record of Discussion of the Interaction between NHRC, India and the UN Special Rapporteur on Extrajudicial, Summary or Arbitrary Executions held on 22 March 2012. Accessed at: http://nhrc.nic.in/Documents/Reports/Record%20Note-%20UN%20Spl.Rapporteur%20on%20Extra-Judicial%20Powers.pdf

33 ibid., p.8.

34 ibid., p.10.

35 ibid., p. 15.

is individual officers who have overstepped the limits of their power/authority."[36]

The mind simply boggles to think that these are the views of a body not only created to safeguard the rights of ordinary citizens, but, in fact, to reassure them that their rights would be safeguarded.

As a link between the State and citizens, the NHRC has chosen to ally itself firmly with the state. To say that the lure of the sprawling offices in Lutyens' Delhi and the red beacon cars beckons the NHRC folks into the fold of the State may be crude. However, the number of retired bureaucrats, police officers and judges who crowd the Commission perpetuate the statist ideology and blunt the edge of its potentialities – despite the limiting nature of the NHRC Act – even when presented with a chance.

In practice, this procedure means that the number of encounter deaths that will be scrutinized diligently for excess will be miniscule.

There have no doubt been some convictions of police officers involved in killings; but those have been the result of relentless pursuit of justice by private citizens. It demands a tenacity that won't fissure and crumble under the collective weight of the System. And chances are even dimmer if those killed are labeled 'terrorists'. Staying the judgement of the AP High Court, the then Chief Justice of the Supreme Court – now the chairperson of the NHRC – said: "We can't fully endorse the judgement... If we have to accept what you say then all police officers involved in the Mumbai terror attack of November 26, 2008 should face criminal charges."

---

36 ibid., p.11.

Why the Ishrat Jahan Case Frightens Our Commentators[1]

On a September morning in 1995, Jaswant Singh Khalra was washing his car outside his Amritsar home. His wife had just left for the library where she worked.

Khalra had spent the last few months perusing the cremation records of the three crematoria in Amritsar, reflecting on the vast quantities of wood that had been purchased, travelling around the countryside, speaking to families whose sons had gone missing, peering at the death and birth registries in the municipal office, meeting with doctors whose task it was to conduct post mortems at the civil hospitals, and comparing these with news reports on encounter killings. There was only one conclusion he could reach. That men, whose numbers ran into thousands, had been burnt to cinders in these cremation grounds. Their bodies sometimes piled one atop each oth-

1 This essay was written in response to a series of articles that appeared in July 2013, when the CBI investigation into the Ishrat Jahan encounter began to point towards some officers in the Intelligence Bureau.

er. Khalra's enquiries had hardly gone unnoticed. He had been warned several times, in particular by the Tarn Taran SSP, Ajit Singh Sandhu, who had threatened to disappear him.

As he washed his car that morning, a Maruti van glided into the street, and armed commandos of the Punjab police pulled him in. His body was never recovered.

More than two years later, Special Police Officer Kuldeep Singh gave a statement to the CBI – which had been directed by the Supreme Court to investigate Khalra's disappearance and his findings of the dead and disappeared – that Khalra had been held secretly at the Jhabal police station and had been interrogated at the home of SSP Sandhu by KPS Gill. Kuldeep Singh testified that Khalra was shot dead in the police station on the evening of 28 October and his body dumped in the Harike canal. The killing was followed by a night of revelry at the irrigation department guest house. SSP Sandhu and KPS Gill were guests of honour.

Piara Singh whose Maruti van had been requisitioned for this operation by the Jhabal police station in September, deposed before the CBI. Kikkar Singh, who had been held in the Jhabal police station in late October also testified that he had been witness to Khalra's torture at the police station.

But then, the CBI dropped its star witnesses pleading that their statements were not substantiated by material evidence. Kikkar Singh was implicated in five criminal cases. Kuldeep Singh was forced to lodge a case of bribery against Khalra's widow.

The grisliness of this dark phase of history, when a brutal force hunted down men – sometimes active militants, but also their former school mates or playmates, neighbours, cousins, brothers, fathers who had never taken up arms – in the fields and the villages, in the darkness of film theatres and in the market squares in broad day light, has been chronicled in the report, *Reduced to Ashes*. Prepared by the comrades of Jaswant Khalra, this report results from the unmet promise of Supreme Court-directed inquiry into mass disappearances and deaths when Khalra's widow filed a writ of habeas corpus about her disappeared husband. A well-read man, Shekhar Gupta, is bound to have read it. Why then did he ask, nay taunt, "But nobody asked how many suspected terrorists they [Punjab police] put through 'due process' ".[2]

He knew surely that they asked. And paid for it with their lives.

> And when questions were raised about fake encounters of killings of innocents, the entire government system colluding in never letting the truth out, even when the Supreme Court had wanted it.

Shekhar Gupta writes this with a sense of nostalgia. For the lost times when the system worked to frustrate every move to uncover the truth. The Congress which signed the license to kill; the Akalis who promised to institute a Truth Commission into mass disappearances but reneged when they came to power; the BJP which dared anyone to touch the 'heroes' of the anti-insurgency ops; the CBI which let the inquiry collapse quietly; the NHRC which was tasked with uncovering the extent of mass crimes but settled for Rupees one lakh each for families for 18 disappeared; the security establishment whose symbol Gill became. (Tavleen Singh was doing exactly what she is doing now: railing against "the human rights wallahs"). How they all worked together like a well-oiled machine, bound by the pact of silence. The pact of the State against

---

2 "Body Politics" by Shekhar Gupta, *Indian Express*, 06 July 2013. http://www.indianexpress.com/news/body-politics/1138181/

its people; the pact between the political rulers and the agencies. The pact of impunity as national security.

The Ishrat Jahan case threatened, albeit briefly, to seriously damage that pact and the privileges of impunity that accrue from it. Senior editors of apparently liberal persuasion, columnists, commentators, security experts, were therefore all out in full force. Some were downright crude. The poster boy of police reforms, seen as a panacea to all that afflicts our police forces, Prakash Singh, wrote that human rights of terrorists (no, he hasn't heard of the terms 'alleged' or 'suspect') have to be circumscribed by societal rights. If this is not seditious, what is? This outright and brazen call to violate the Constitution and the Law of the land, which he must presumably have sworn to in service.

And then there were those who have made sophistry their trade. Their arguments usually began thus: killing and torture is bad. It's terrible that Ishrat was killed. No, encounters are not permissible. But.

Gupta writes: "You can safely say that our intelligence past hasn't exactly been either ineffective or incompetent, nor would it pass with flying colours if subjected to the legal/moral scrutiny of the Ishrat Jahan case." And Praveen Swami rued that "Our Intelligence won't survive it".[3]

And *that* is the problem. More than anything else, it is Ishrat's sweet, demure 19-year-old innocence that holds up the mirror to the grotesque vision of the national security state. The exacting moral and legal standards that Ishrat Jahan demands are simply an adherence to the principles of the Constitution. Is it too much to ask for?

---

3 "Ishrat Jahan Case: Intelligence won't survive the Investigation" by Praveen Swami, *Firstpost.com*, 08 July 2013. Access at: http://www.firstpost.com/india/ishrat-jahan-case-intelligence-wont-survive-the-investigation-939229.html

Apparently, it is. If you thought that the Constitution was the basis of your Republic; if you believed that the rule of law underlies the idea of Republic, you have been utterly wrong. We were now told that the pillars of our Republic have been and will be: "Gun-running. Bribery. Killing." One could direct the author to an undergraduate text of Political Science so that he could brush up his understanding of 'Republic'. But one would do so, if the author suffered from ignorance rather than hubris. "Only those who never exercise power have the luxury of moral pieties", he said, placing himself firmly on the side of those who exercise power and lack morality. The powerful will run the country according to an amoral pragmatism, and those who lack the power, who will be at the receiving end of this power, can feel squeamish all they want. It makes no difference.

The same author has in the past also advocated torture.

> Evidence of the successes or failures of torture is, of course, hard to come by. Few will confess to engaging in torture – and the testimony of those who must necessarily be treated with caution, either way. For as long as torture remains illegal, and hidden away, there's simply no empirically-robust way of knowing whether it works or not.[4]

The clamour for legalizing torture is hardly new or novel. And it often comes wrapped in a moral or a higher philosophical foil. The ticking bomb has been presented as a moral dilemma but has been called out for the bluff that it is.[5]

---

4 "From the US to India: Is Torture alright if it curbs Terror?" by Praveen Swami, *Firstpost.com*. 19 April 2013. Access at: http://www.firstpost.com/world/from-the-us-to-india-is-torture-alright-if-it-curbs-terror-711878.html

5 "Liberalism, Torture, and the Ticking Bomb" by David Luban, *Virginia Law Review*, Vol. 91: 1425.

But to say that it should be legalized in order that we may 'robustly' empirically measure its success – or failure – takes it to another level. How is the success rate to be measured? Through careful calibration of pain induced and the responses evoked? Or by drawing graphs and charts with pain and responses as variables?

Not too far back in history, we have indeed had these experiments: the Nazi regime was notorious for its medical pain trials; and immediately following the end of Second World War, the US Navy sanctioned an interrogation research called Project Chatter (experiments involving injecting drugs which would bring forth chatter), which was the precursor to a string of such experiments.

It was said to be involuntary but 'painless' way of eliciting information. The Forensics Science Laboratory (FSL) at Bangalore had been conducting its own Project Chatter for years till a scandal dethroned the notorious Dr. Narco (Malini) and a Supreme Court judgement brought it to a grinding halt.[6] More painful ways can be found in the torture chambers of the ATSs and Grey Hounds, with their paraphernalia and contraptions of belts, chairs, gases, insects and screw drivers.

Project Chatter used human beings and animals to experiment upon. Narco analysis, rarely recognized as torture, reduced humans to the animal state.

Speaking of animals, a new phrase has just been introduced to the existing discourse on extra judicial violence: "controlled killing". I have little doubt that the process which Shekhar Gupta describes –"where you use moles and plants to lure your targets into a trap and then put them away" – existed and still thrives.

---

6 *Selvi & Others vs State of Karnataka & Anr*, Supreme Court, Bench: KG Balakrishnan, RV Raveendran, JM Panchal, 5 May 2010.

Swami, with his penchant for theatricality, dramatizes the scenario by introducing his own cast: c1 and c2, unnamed operatives of the Lashkar forced into submission and cooperation by the IB, which culminated in the killing of Ishrat Jahan.

But the new terminology itself sought to rehabilitate extra judicial violence into the domain of the acceptable, the normal. By placing controlled killing in a grey zone between due process and fake encounter, Gupta attempted to give it a veneer of respectability, even a faux legality. It is not impulsive violence of the undisciplined. It is carried out with precision, accuracy, planning. It is violence in good faith and for the greater good.

Even for someone familiar with literature on violence, death sqauds and genocides, 'controlled killing' will be an odd, unfamiliar phrase. And that is because it has never been used for human beings. It is a term used to describe a less brutal, more humane way of slaughtering animals and poultry. It is a technique that is advocated by PETA over the electronic immobilization traditionally followed by the American poultry industry.

Extra judicial violence must be condoned, it is being drilled into our ears, because of the collapse of our judicial system.

This is an argument that's not new. It was deployed to sugar coat the disappearances in Punjab – and deaths, the bodies fished out from its numerous canals, half eaten by crocodiles, or sometimes just bones, which were washed off as afar as Rajasthan. This argument forgets that Punjab had been placed under an exceptional legal regime – the National Security Act (NSA), AFSPA, and the draconian TADA, which inverted the principles of natural justice shifting the burden of proof to the accused, allowed admission of custodial confessions, secret trials even in the absence of the accused.

That such few militants were prosecuted and convicted arose from the preference of the security forces for quick fix gun justice over the more painstaking investigative and police work.

"Law, order and justice, aren't the same things. In war, sometimes one can have the one or the others", says Swami.

It reminds one of the legendary line scribbled on shops that sell 'import reject' cloth material: "*fashion ke is daur men guarantee ki umeed na karein*" (Please do not expect guarantee in this era of fashion). The guarantee of Constitutional safeguards has been sacrificed to the reigning fashion of war on terror.

But it's a war in which norms of war apply no longer. If it's a war, call it war and apply Geneva Conventions. But it's a war unlike any other, we are told. It is an unconventional war. A war in which a preferred method of putting away poultry will be offered to us as a substitute for due process.

Our abhorrence for cruelty is very much a rather recent phenomenon. The moral repugnance against torture is neither trans-historical nor universal. (So, how exactly does Swami's comparison of humans with chimpanzees complicate the moral debate is unclear)[7]. It has evolved out of the experiences of human history, particularly those of the last century. The indivisibility and primacy of human life emerged in a context ravaged by war and conflict, not a state of normalcy. That human life was precious and the right to life non-negotiable *even* in times of war, and *especially* in times of war was a lesson that the world learnt as it emerged from the dust, smoke and debris of Second World War.

---

7 According to Swami, the fact that chimpanzees engage in cruelty – or torture – could give us good reason not to condemn it outrightly.

So this refrain of dire times calling for dire strategies, including torture and extra judicial violence, sweetly labeled as "excesses" is vacuous, even if it is in vogue these days.

To try and trace Ishrat Jahan's appeal in public imagination as either a result of Narendra Modi's persona, which evokes polarized responses, or to Congress' petty and opportunist politicization of the issue – as many commentators did – is simply a desperate attempt, and even more, a fervent wish, that Ishrat Jahan case does not culminate in the absolute wreckage of the idea of the security state and the pact that sustains it.

What is being asked, shamefully, even if cleverly, in the name of a legal framework and oversight of intelligence agencies, is the legalization of extra judicial violence: torture, killing, maiming. Gupta ends his article with a plea: "Constitutional State even creates a legal mechanism to kill without due process, but assigns accountability". Accountability to whom? To the politicians who condone? In the end, his is an appeal for the resurrection of the pact.

Like the torture memos – which were produced by a Law Professor in the US at the behest of the Bush regime to circumvent domestic laws and international treaties, to protect the torturers and killers from law – these commentaries erode our collective commitment towards the Constitution and rule of law.

This will spell the end of the Republic. Only an empty shell will survive, a security state bereft of any values and ethics.

Crime and Punishment

An RTI enquiry in 2011 revealed that the Delhi Police Special Cell's conviction rate was a paltry 30 per cent. Nearly 70 per cent of the accused it chargehseeted over the previous five years were acquitted for want of credible evidence. Do these figures tell us something? A news story in a leading English daily bemoaned this trifling record and quoted a senior police officer attributing this to the fact that "police sometimes get tangled in cross evidences and it becomes tough when you rely more on circumstantial evidences".[1] This evokes the image of a bumbling policeman, reminiscent almost of Jacques Clouseau, tripping over reams and strings of evidences, in an impossible attempt to build a watertight case against the villains. But Special Cell couldn't be farther from this sort of cute sloppiness.

---

1 "70 % Acquittals in Special Cell Cases" by Dwaipayan Ghosh, *Times of India*, 8 October 2011. http://articles.timesofindia.indiatimes.com/2011-10-09/delhi/30259861_1_special-cell-chargesheeted-p-n-aggarwal) accessed on 1st November 2011

These bare statistics of 30-70 must be read in conjunction with court judgments and the track record of the Special Cell itself to arrive at the big picture. It is not shoddy investigative skills – a pardonable offence; or poor infrastructure – a justifiable excuse again – but the simple non-existence of a case that is allowing the accused to secure acquittals. Created in 1986 to tackle terrorism and high profile crime, Special Cell has become a law unto itself, a marauding force, 'encountering' and detaining 'suspects' almost at will. This is not the charge of bleeding heart liberals and human rights wallahs alone, but a fact corroborated by judgment after judgment of the city courts.

There is a nauseating familiarity to the narrative of the Special Cell's busting of terror modules. This is the stream of events as is usually recorded in the FIR: secret information is received by the police about the entry of a dreaded terrorist into Delhi via bus/car/railways to meet an aide to conspire about an attack or pass on arms and ammunition. Losing no time, a party is readied and dispatched to the spot. The police party unsuccessfully entreats civilians to join them as public witnesses. An encounter ensues. The terrorist is apprehended. Cash, arms, and caches of explosives recovered, and the terrorist and the booty displayed suitably in a press conference. Glory invariably follows.

It is only years later, with the accused already having spent years in jail – his business destroyed, his children out of school, and in many cases, family members suffering from severe mental depression – that the truth starts to emerge. This is the terrible truth of illegal detention, torture, extortion and frame-ups.

On 14 June 2005, Moinuddin Dar and Bashir Ahmed Shah travelled to Delhi from Kashmir in connection with their tea business carrying with them about Rupees 4.5

lakh in cash for transactions.[2] As was their custom, the duo stayed in a hotel in Karol Bagh. They befriended two fellow Kashmiris who were booked into a room close to theirs. Two evenings later, when Dar was relaxing in his room and Rehman out with their new friends for dinner at Nizaumddin, there was a knock on the door. Dar found two men at his door, one of them claiming to be Ravinder Tyagi of the Delhi Police Special Branch. The other man was Major Sharma of the Indian Army posted in Kashmir. Dar's nightmare had begun.

Over the next couple of days the four Kashmiri men were detained in the hotel by the police, subjected to torture and indignities and forced to sign blank sheets of paper. Slowly, Tyagi and his men turned the hotel into their private torture chamber collecting thirteen Kashmiris in its rooms. The men were taken to the Dhaula Kuan police station where senior police officers demanded money in lieu of freedom. Nearly two weeks after they were illegally confined in their hotel room, Dar, Bashir and two other men, Saqib Rehman and Nazeer Ahmed Sofi – the last picked up from the Delhi airport when his flight landed from Srinagar on 20 June – were driven to the Police Headquarters. As they got off from the police vehicle, they noted a frenzied media presence – the four were thrust in front of the cameras by a preening Tyagi who claimed to have arrested them after an encounter on the National Highway 8 near the international airport. A press photo of a smooth-looking Tyagi and dazed-looking accused, separated only by a row of seized arms and explosives, survived. This public moment of glory was to be one of the key evidences that would nail the lie of police claims.

The prosecution's story was that on 27 June 2005, a secret informer (but of course!) apprised Ravinder Tya-

2 Personal interview with Moinuddin Dar.

gi – then posted as sub inspector in Special Branch of Dhaula Kuan – of the nefarious designs of two Kashmiri terrorists, Masood and Zahid.[3] Tyagi asked his source to develop this information further. After a brief lull, on 1 July, the secret informer resurfaced with the valuable news that the two terrorists along with two associates, ferrying a huge consignment of arms and ammunition, were headed into Delhi from Jaipur in a blue Tata Indica (HR26S0440). Tyagi led a police party and sat waiting on the national Highway and voila, along came the blue Tata Indica in the early hours of 2 July. After a chase – involving cross fire and hurling of hand grenades – worthy of a Bollywood potboiler, the terrorists were apprehended. Zahid was none other than Dar.

The deposition of the star witness Ravinder Tyagi crumbled under the scrutiny of the judge. Tyagi could not reveal to the court his secret informer – nor reply to why he felt no urgency to inform either the IB or his seniors about the impending terror strike. The judge firmly held that no one could be convicted on the basis of secret information which could be not be "tested on the touchstone of the cross examination by the accused."[4] The Court dismantled the case screw by screw, bolt by bolt.

An army combatant uniform was ostensibly seized from the 'terrorists' and traced by the police to a tailor in Gopinath Bazar in Delhi Cantt. The police rushed off to verify this in the official vehicle (No. DL1LD1264) and did indeed discover the tailor plying his trade in the market. The tailor when produced in the court not only identified Dar but also admitted to selling the uniform

3 Based on *State versus Saqib Rehman and Others* (SC No. 24/10); Shri Virender Bhat, ASJ, Dwarka Courts, New Delhi; judgement delivered on 02.02. 2011.

4 *Ibid.*, p. 29.

to him. So far so good. The log record of the vehicle in which the police party had paid the tailor a visit showed no movement on the said day; the vehicle had remained parked all day at the police station.[5] But never mind that – it could have been a simple mistake – perhaps they clean forgot to make this important entry in the log book. Never mind also that the tailor sometimes claimed that Dar had purchased a readymade uniform and at other times said that the uniform had been made to measure on Dar's order. He must have, after all, prepared several of these uniforms for scores of clients and it would be unfair to expect him to remember the precise details of all of those. But certainly, it was very odd that the tailor turned out to be a stock witness of the police, appearing and giving evidence in many cases on behalf of the police (odd also how criminals and terrorists made a beeline for the same tailor when they needed fake army uniforms). On closer examination of his testimony, the tailor conceded that he operated his shop from a pavement which left him at the mercy of police and municipality officials, and false testimonies were his way of paying *hafta* to the police. It was in fact he, who had been summoned to the Dhaula Kuan PS where Dar was duly exhibited to him.[6]

A sketch of the Palam airport was apparently recovered from the pocket of Dar – a point used by the prosecution as proof of the terrorist conspiracy. The court, however, noted that for the sketch to be kept in the pocket, it would have to be folded more than twice. The fact that there was a single fold longitudinally with no creases suggested that the sketch had been planted as an afterthought. Also, the police upon recovering the sketch made no attempt to either corroborate Dar's handwriting on the

5 *Ibid.*, p. 66.

6 *Ibid.*, p. 67.

sketch, nor to inform the Palam airport authorities about a possible terror attack.[7] The Tata Indica, which was supposedly the vehicle of choice of the alleged terrorists, was shown to be stolen and an FIR produced in this regard. The FIR turned out to be in fact about another car. Moreover, the records showed that the car was registered with the transport authority months after it was supposedly misappropriated – leading the court to conclude that "Tata Indica car was planted and merely used as a tool to falsely implicate the accused persons in this case."[8]

But best of all – and the most brazen if you will – was the press conference on the day of the "encounter". The police merrily forgot to account for it in their case. Sub Inspector Mahender Singh deposed in the court that he "took the accused along with him from the encounter site to P.S. Kapasahera at 10.45 a.m." from where he reached Hotel Baba Continental, Karol Bagh, at 12 noon, left from there at 1.30 p.m. for the Patiala House Courts."[9] So when did the press conference take place? There was no press conference, the prosecution firmly responded. But for the photograph of Tyagi strutting his catch published in a Hindi daily which was preserved by the defence.

Circumstantial evidence, says a senior police officer, is the bane of prosecution, allowing many accused to walk free. But what of forged evidence and circumstances spun out of thin air? And don't forget the figure of Major Sharma who accompanied Tyagi's team to the hotel in Karol Bagh. Sharma belonged to Army intelligence and had been posted in Kashmir for six years and subsequently transferred to Delhi as Lt. Colonel. Dar and another co-accused Abdul Majeed Bhatt had worked for

---

7 *Ibid.*, p. 63.

8 Ibid., p. 74.

9 Ibid., p. 78

the surrender of several militants for the police in Kashmir. Sharma got the wind of it and sensing the possibility of awards urged the duo to arrange for surrender before him.[10] Stung by the rejection of his offer, he colluded with Tyagi to implicate these men in this charade of a terror plot – a point not unobserved by the court:

> They [accused] are totally innocent and have been framed in this case by the aforesaid four police officers in order to achieve their personal gains and/or to settle petty personal scores, be that at the behest of one Major Sharma, whose attempts to persuade accused Gulam Moinuddin Dar to work for him in getting the militants surrendered in Kashmir were spurned by him (Gulam Moinuddin Dar) or to earn undue honours or awards for themselves.[11]

This is by no means the solitary case of manipulated evidence and motivated investigation – nor a rare instance of cynical complicity between Intelligence and counter insurgency forces. Many would be familiar with the case of Irshad Ali and Md. Qamar, informers for the IB, who tired of risking their lives, refused to infiltrate a Kashmiri insurgent organization as demanded by IB officers and were punished for their stubbornness by being abducted by the Special Cell – and surprise, surprise, Ravinder Tyagi played a key role here in this operation as well – tortured unnecessarily for months and then produced before the media as Al Badr terrorists caught with arms and explosives, getting off a bus at Mukarba Chowk on the Delhi border.[12] The duo's telephone call records showed that they had been long in touch with IB; the bus tickets produced before the court were of a day previous to that on which Irshad and Qamar were allegedly arrested. In

10 Personal interview with Moinuddin Dar.

11 *State versus Saqib Rehman and Others*, p. 109.

12 Trail of Terror Cops" by Nirmalangshu Mukherji, *Revolutionary Democracy*, Vol. XIV, No. 2, September 2008.

its closure report, CBI, which had been directed by the High Court to investigate the case, called for prosecution of three officers of the Special Cell, including Vinay Tyagi, Subhash Vats, and of course, Ravinder Tyagi for lying under oath and creating "false" evidence, among other serious offences.[13] This was not all. Inspector Santosh Kumar, the CBI investigating officer fearing for his safety following threats, moved an application in the court of additional sessions judge seeking protection from Sub Inspector Vinay Tyagi who was threatening him with dire consequences.[14]

In 2005, the Special Cell emerged heroic after averting a major attack on the Indian Military Academy (IMA), Dehradun, by apprehending four terrorists following a fierce encounter in Uttam Nagar in South West Delhi.[15] There was as usual the mandatory press conference where the prize catches were displayed for the media and the brave Special Cell officers vied to be photographed with the 'terrorists' they had nabbed.

---

13 "CBI indicts Special Cell of Delhi Police", *Hindustan Times*, Nov. 16, 2008. http://www.hindustantimes.com/StoryPage/Print/351960.aspx

14 "Special Cell Cop threatens CBI Sleuth", by Aman Sharma, *Mail Today*, 15 January 2009. http://indiatoday.intoday.in/story/Special+cell+cop+threatens+CBI+sleuth/1/25317.html

15 "Slain Militants had Plans to Attack IMA", *Tribune News Service*, 6 March 2005 aand "3 LeT militants killed in Police Encounter" *Times of India*, 5 March 2005. http://articles.timesofindia.indiatimes.com/2005-03-05/delhi/27847966_1_three-militants-police-encounter-special-cell. The encounter – and following it, the arrests, were accepted as the undisputed truth in the media. One commentator linked this "abortive attack on cadets at the Indian Military Academy in Dehra Dun" to an alleged dreaded kingpin of Lashkar–e Tayyaba, bin Aziz. See "Harvest of Hate" by Praveen Swami, *Frontline*, Volume 23 - Issue 05: Mar. 11-24, 2006. http://www.hindu.com/fline/fl2305/stories/20060324005001900.htm

Five years after they were sent to jail for being Laskhar-e Tayyaba (LeT) militants planning a daring attack on IMA, the Court ruled that they had been set up by the Special Cell.[16] It was a familiar tale of lies, misrepresentation of facts, and contradictions, which could not stand the scrutiny of cross examination.[17] The remittances by one of the accused, Haroon, through Western Union were shown to be the monies used by LeT to fund the IMA campaign. It turned out to be repayment of a loan to a generous uncle who financed Haroon's travel to Singapore. The email transcripts between Haroon and his Pakistani handler were proved to be fabrications by the police. The recoveries from the home of Iftikhar, a student of Biotechnology at an Institute in Dehradun, demonstrated in the Special Cell's view his deep involvement in the conspiracy. Ignore for a moment the Special Cell norm of preparing a seizure list in the absence of any independent public witness and focus on two key items seized: a pass to the IMA parade and a diary containing inflammatory passages from the Quran and a note declaring vengeance for Gujarat 2002.

The pass turned out to be five months old, the parade already over long before the busting of the IMA 'terror plot'. More interesting was the fact that all officers of the Special Cell developed amnesia in court about which of them had visited Dehradun to conduct the raid. Neither could they remember whether the revenge note was writ-

---

16 "Delhi Court Acquits Four in IMA Attack Conspiracy", *Times of India*, 8 January 2010. http://articles.timesofindia.indiatimes.com/2010-01-08/delhi/28137749_1_ima-indian-military-academy-acquits

17 See the reports in "Terror that's Wasn't" by Brijesh Pandey, *Tehelka Magazine*, Vol. 7, Issue 08, 27 February, 2010. http://www.tehelka.com/story_main43.asp?filename=Ne270210terror_that.asp

ten out in Hindi or English. The court was inclined to listen to Iftikhar's charge that he had been forced to scribble out the revenge note in his diary next to the passages from Quran (which were not in any way inflammatory). Perhaps they were inspired by the Maharashtra ATS which has perfected and peddled the Revenge theory so well that it has acquired the currency of an axiom.

Maharashtra ATS is not the only inspiration. 9/11 fascinates the Special Cell just as much. Imran Kirmani, an aeronautical engineer, was picked up from his home in November 2006 and presented before eager reporters as the sensational LeT catch planning a "9/11 type strike in Delhi".[18] In October this year, the Court dismissed the flimsy 'secret information' which, no surprises by now, Ravinder Tyagi, had received about the plot. Moreover, there were others in the Special Cell, sub inspectors RS Shehrawat and Ramesh Lamba, as well as ACP Sanjeev Kumar Yadav, who claimed in court to be recipients of this valuable secret information. The FSL report contradicted the Special cell claim that RDX was seized from Kirmani. The court noted fudging of records, namely the *ruqqa*, which was originally recorded to be of two pages but which mysteriously expanded to seven pages when attached with the chargesheet. It was strange also, commented the court that having apprehended a dreaded LeT terrorist, the Special Cell made no attempt to determine their hideout.[19]

---

18 "RDX Seized in Delhi: Two Arrested", *The Hindu*, 23 November 2006. The leader to the report said: "Leads to seizure of 1.65 kg of RDX, timers and Rs. 4.5 lakh. Police suspect that the outfit had planned to carry out a major terrorist strike." http://www.hindu.com/2006/11/23/stories/2006112314650100.htm.

19 "Held for '9-11 type' plot, no case 4 years later" Muzamil Jaleel, *Indian Express*, 03 October 2011. http://www.indianexpress.com/news/held-for-9-11type-plot-no-case-4-years-later/854879/0

The Special Cell also tried to inject a dose of 9/11 in the Delhi blasts 2008 case by alleging that one of the accused, Shahzad, apparently a trained pilot, was the head of the aerial module of Indian Mujahideen.[20] But their theory crash-landed rather quickly after it was discovered that Shahzad had never ever enrolled in a flying course, and had zero flying skills.[21]

So, difficulty of tying down slippery circumstantial evidence – or simple frame ups which can't pass the test of evidence and law? The Special Cell hopes that the burden of evidence can be considerably lowered in cases of terrorism, where patriotism, national security and even prejudice can be called upon as dependable alibis. When asked for evidence to prove the implication of Md. Salman in the Delhi blasts case by the judge, the public prosecutor continually spoke of the dangers terrorism posed to the country. When asked how Salman's innocuous telephone conversations demonstrated his guilt, the public prosecutor invoked the climate of fear created by terrorism and how India was waging a war on terror. He, no doubt, hoped that war on terror would be viewed by the court as legitimate substitute for evidence.[22]

---

20 "UP cops nab IM Terrorist planning Aerial Strike" by Pervez Iqbal Siddiqui, *Times of India*, 2 February 2010. http://timesofindia.indiatimes.com/city/delhi/UP-cops-nab-IM-terrorist-planning-aerial-strike/articleshow/5525935.cms. The story reported that "Shehzad…had undergone a training to fly planes from an institute in Bangalore and had surfaced as a leader of the module designated to execute aerial terror attacks." See also http://zeenews.india.com/news/nation/nabbed-im-operative-was-planning-air-attacks_600855.html

21 *Mail Today*, 6 February 2010.

22 "Suspected IM Man discharged in 2008 Serial Blasts Case", *Times of India*, 7 February 2010. **http://articles.timesofindia.indiatimes.com/2011-02-07/delhi/28363947_1_serial-blasts-rajiv-mohan-khalil-ansari**. See also "Show me the evidence, says Judge. The

Counter insurgency spawns its own political economy; the promise and prospect of promotions, cash awards, public adulation, glorification by a pliant media, all work to lubricate a machinery which transforms innocents into terrorists. It should come as no surprise that the ascent of city's encounter specialists – SS Rathi, LN Rao and Rajbir Singh – in police hierarchy was swift, all receiving out of turn promotions and rapidly reaching the rank of ACPs; in fact Rajbir Singh became the only officer to be promoted to ACP rank in a mere thirteen years after joining as sub inspector in 1982.[23] Their dizzy rise was facilitated by the suffering of men like Dar and Bashir Ahmed, and countless others whom they claimed to have shot down in difficult crossfire ops.

Remember the encounter at Connaught Place in 1997? Two businessmen were gunned down point blank by these brave men of the Special Cell led by SS Rathi. Or Ansal Plaza in 2002? Within hours of gunning down of two 'Kashmiri terrorists' in the basement of this upscale shopping centre on Diwali eve, the then Home Minister LK Advani rushed to the encounter site to bathe in the afterglow of the glories of Special Cell's operation. (And the police used his presence to seal the authenticity of the 'encounter').[24]

Prosecution is able to produce none! Md. Salman discharged from the 2008 Delhi Blasts Case!" http://www.countercurrents.org/jtsa050211.htm

23 "Our Encounter Specialists", *Indian Express*, 18 October 2007. http://www.expressindia.com/latest-news/our-encounter-specialists/229578/

24 "Delhi Police under Fire after Ansal Plaza Shootout" by Pratyush Kanth and Siddharth Srivastav, *Times of India*, 5 November 2002. http://articles.timesofindia.indiatimes.com/2002-11-05/delhi/27307307_1_three-diaries-ansal-plaza-delhi-police

The jingoistic hype created by the Ansal Plaza encounter was punctured by a good doctor, Dr. Hari Krishna, who contradicted the police story that two terrorists had driven into the shopping complex in a Maruti 800; instead, he said, he had seen the two men, barely able to stand or walk, being almost dragged by the Special Cell officers and then shot in cold blood. For years, Dr. Hari Krishna was hounded and threatened: old cases, long settled were raked up, his reputation tarnished, his claims of being present at the site of encounter dismissed by doctoring the records of his mobile phone through collusion with a cellular company.[25]

But who shall bell the cat? The courts have on numerous occasions passed strictures against the Special Cell, noting especially its predatory ways, even asking for filing of FIRs against them and departmental enquiries (as in the case of Dar and Bashir Ahmed) or directed for their prosecution (as in the Al Badr frame up and CP encounter). Despite repeated offences, Special Cell officers remain the darlings of the Delhi Police top brass receiving their protection, patronage and legal aid. In every single case where action was called for against them, appeals were filed to avert prosecution. Additional DCP of the Special Cell, Ravi Shankar, one of the key officers chosen to lead the investigation in the Delhi High Court blast of mid-September 2011 was found to be extorting money by

---

25 The NHRC issued directives to the Police to ensure the safety of the eye witness but the harassment continued unabated, with. PUDR wring to the NHRC to intervene as late as 2007. http://www.pudr.org/content/letter-nhrc-harassment-ansal-plaza-shoot-out-witness. Dr. Hari Krishna also shared his experiences in a presentation at the release of the report, *Batla House 'Encounter': Unanswered Questions*, (JTSA), Jamia Millia Islamia, 20 February 2009.

threatening to implicate people in false cases.[26] Shankar and his co-accused appealed against the chief metropolitan magistrate's order seeking the filing of an FIR in a city court and indeed were able to wrest a stay.[27]

While as individuals they have right to legal recourse, one must seriously ask how the State continues to back them in their legal battles. The sentencing of Rathi and nine of his men who were found guilty of killing in cold blood in the CP encounter was repeatedly appealed against and was finally upheld by the Supreme Court in May 2011 – thirteen years after they carried out the execution.[28] It was only in 2009 that a Delhi court allowed Dr. Hari Krishna's evidence to be recorded. But by then, the prime witness had battled years of intimidation and the chief accused, ACP Rajbir Singh, had been killed in shady circumstances by a property dealer in Gurgaon amidst talk of unseemly land deals. Whatever the truth of these allegations, one thing was certain: the Special Cell's elite position and wide powers allowed it to subvert the rule of law, turning it into a rampaging monster.

---

26 Audio CD blew lid over Special Cell Extortion Racket", *Indian Express*, 15 September 2011. http://www.indianexpress.com/news/audio-cd-blew-lid-off-special-cell-extortion/846934/. And "Crime Branch Cop in the Dock over Extortion", *Times of India*, 14 September 2011. http://articles.timesofindia.indiatimes.com/2011-09-14/delhi/30154068_1_special-cell-mcoca-case-delhi-police

27 "Court stays FIR against Special Cell Personnel in Extortion Case", *Indian Express*, 23 September 2011. http://www.indianexpress.com/news/court-stays-fir-against-special-cell-personn/850450/

28 "Fake Encounter Case: Supreme Court Upholds Life Sentence of Rathi", *Jagran Post*, 2 May 2011. http://post.jagran.com/fake-encounter-case-supreme-court-upholds-life-sentence-of-rathi-9-others-cops-1304350487

Salman was discharged. Moinuddin Dar and Bashir Ahmed were acquitted, as were Irshad Ali and Qamar, as did Iftikhar, Haroon and Kirmani gain their freedom.[29] But after brutal torture, public ignominy and condemnation, humiliating press conferences, years in prison, loss of employment and businesses, broken families, the ever-present terror of the police, and fear as constant companion.

Why does the government – which consistently blocked all enquiries into the Batla House encounter, which expressed satisfaction with the reports placed by senior police officers, on which basis it dismissed, indeed violated the NHRC procedural requirement for a magisterial inquiry – stand with these repeat offenders of the Delhi police? Ravinder Tyagi and Investigating Officer Mahinder Singh filed two writs in the High Court: one, seeking the overturning of acquittal of Dar and others, and the second asking for a stay on criminal proceedings against them. Indeed, in response to an RTI application filed by Jamia Teachers Solidarity Association (JTSA) seeking information if the court's order of filing an FIR and departmental inquiry had been initiated, the Delhi Police responded that they had neither filed an FIR nor initiated a departmental inquiry as the police officers had appealed against the order.[30]

---

29 KPS Gill's South Asia Terrorism Portal (SATP), a one-stop documentation of terror attacks since 1997 continues to happily list all those acquitted as terrorists, and all proven frame-ups as terror attacks. See http://www.satp.org/satporgtp/countries/india/database/Delhi_Incidents.htm

30 JTSA's application was filed on 23.03.2011 under the RTI Act 2005. A communication dated 06.04.2011 (No. 2818 (701)/DIC/SWD) was received from the office of the Additional Deputy Commissioner of Police-I Cum PIO, South West District, Dwarka, New Delhi.

Had not the Commissioner of Police read the verdict of the court which blew the prosecution case to smithereens? Did the senior authority in the Delhi Police feel no moral obligation to conduct an inquiry in the aftermath of such a damning indictment of its decorated officers? Are they unaware of the CBI closure report which indicts the Special Cell for falsely framing innocents? Have they paused to ask how the Special Cell manages to produce explosives and vast amounts of cash to be displayed at press conferences? Is it the case of a few rogue officers? Rathi and his band of nine merry shooters continued to serve in the police even when they were convicted by the lower court on the ground "that their appeals against such conviction are pending before the superior courts," an outraged High Court noted seeking the response of the MHA.[31]

If these were mere personal transgressions of a few individuals then surely they would have been suspended and taken off duty years ago. Instead what they received were medals, rapid promotions and a virtual license to kill.

One suspects that the matter is deeper than that. The Special Cell – or the various ATS and STF for that matter – represent our impatience with due process of law and the increasing impunity afforded to those we see as custodians of national security. They are to the police forces what AFSPA is to the army: enjoying utter impunity with almost a blanket immunity from prosecution, or even departmental reprimands. Just a week after the Ansal Plaza encounter, inaugurating the Asia Pacific Human Rights conference, Prime Minister Vajpayee was advocating the erosion of human rights as a necessary corollary to the

---

31 "CP Encounter: Why wasn't ACP Dismissed, asks HC", PTI, 13 January 2011. http://news.outlookindia.com/items.aspx?artid=708354

war on terror: "we have sometimes to take tough decisions, even infringing some of our freedoms and abridging some of our human rights temporarily, to firmly counter terrorism...."[32] A sentiment echoed by former chief justice of the Supreme Court and current chairperson of the National Human Rights Commission when he deemed encounters as "unavoidable sometimes ... the law and order problem is increasing. Criminals are taking law into their hands, attacking even the police. Police have to take control of the situation."[33]

The real cause for concern should not be the low rate of conviction in the cases 'cracked' by the Special Cell – but the appalling lack of prosecution of the officers of Special Cell and the near total absence of any departmental inquiry or action against them.

---

32 *The Hindu*, 12 November 2002.

33 "Is Justice Balakrishnan holding a devil's brief?", statement by the Asian Legal Resource Centre, 30 July 2010. http://www.humanrights.asia/news/alrc-news/ALRC-STM-004-2010

Sinful Liberals and the Investigative Bias

In October 2012, Jamia Teachers' Solidarity Association brought out its report, *Framed, Damned, Acquitted,* chronicling in detail how Delhi Police's Special Cell implicated innocents – former militants, police informers, businessmen, and just ordinary, unlucky men – as terrorists. It is one of the few documents that lends evidentiary credence to the widespread sense amongst Muslims that they are being targeted in the war against terror. Apologists for the police and investigative agencies however do not tire of contesting its conclusions, namely that there is a systemic and systematic bias against minorities when it comes to terror investigations. What bias, they ask?[1]

Could they be echoing the sentiments of a judge of the Allahabad High Court, who less than two decades after India gained independence, noted, that "in the entire

1 "Liberals are Compromising the War against Jihadi Terror" by Praveen Swami, Firstpost.com, 16 March 2013. Access at: http://www.firstpost.com/india/liberals-are-compromising-the-war-against-jihadi-terror-663797.html

country there is not another criminal force whose misdeeds can come anywhere near the list of crimes of that organised body called the Indian Police force."[2] Do they mean, that our extraordinarily brutal police force is even-handed in its application of cruelty across the spectrum of our citizenry, and is not especially biased against the Muslims, or Dalits, adivasis and so on?

But one doubts very much if this is what these commentators mean. Confronted by a long list of acquittals in terror trials, they argue, that this is a result simply of incompetence, or stretched resources. Nothing in the way these investigations are carried out or prosecuted seems to them to suggest prejudice against Muslims. Comparable data of falling conviction rates in murder, but especially rape, is cited as proof that it is poor investigative skills and other mundane matters rather than any bias that seems to be at the root of the acquittals of terror suspects.[3]

And further, this unnecessary fuss over communal profiling or targeting is 'compromising the war against jihadi terror'. If only we were to zip up our lips and turn a blind eye to what seems to us as deliberate framing of members of a specific community – we would greatly strengthen the battle against jihadi terror. Our problem, according to Mr. Swami, is that we may have "moved, too easily, from primitive fable to post-modern text, bypassing the stage of evidence-based appraisals altogether."

Just days before we released our report, there were a series of arrests in Bangalore and Hubli, where young men, many of whom were university educated and professionals, were arrested by the Bangalore for conspiring to kill right wing Hindu leaders. News channels and news-

---

2 *India Reporter*, 1964, Vol. 51, pp. 702-8.

3 "A State of Criminal Injustice" by Praveen Swami, *The Hindu*, 22nd October 2012. http://www.thehindu.com/opinion/lead/a-state-of-criminal-injustice/article4019671.ece

papers, vernacular and English alike, delighted in headlines – one more perverse than the other – which confidently spoke about the guilt of those arrested.[4] Six months later, two of those 15 arrested were discharged, while the third, a scientist with Defence Research and Development Organization (DRDO), was released on bail – even as his name did not appear in the chargesheet filed by the NIA, to whom the case had been transferred since then. Upon their release, the three young men spoke movingly of their period of incarceration, the trauma they and their families suffered – but also of the sense of hurt they felt at having been arrested, they suspected, only because they were Muslims.

Plain shortsightedness, felt our leading security expert.

> The facts ... suggest the need for a more nuanced reading of these instances of Muslims who are released for want of evidence and not simply as another case of 'police-led persecution of Muslims'.

He invites us to "test the assumptions against the facts in the Bangalore case". Yes, do lets. (And, er, it is known popularly as the Bangalore Assassination Case, not Bangalore Jihad Case, as Swami calls it.)

> The NIA's charge-sheet outlines perhaps the most ambitious jihadist project since 26/11, and the first Indian case involving online self-radicalisation.

So ambitious was this project that the centerpiece of evidence is an obsolete Berretta pistol, which would have

---

4 Just by way of example, see "Bob Biswas as scribe? Siddiqui's the demure killer mastermind", *Times of India*, 31 August 2012.

been used allegedly to kill the Hindutva leaders and editors.[5]

'Online self radicalization' is a nice sounding phrase, in vogue these days in security study circles.[6] But as theories go, it is dangerous to base them on the shifting quick sand of leaks and sources. Six months ago, journalists who hadn't anticipated the possibility of Muthiur Rehman's discharge were referring to him as "the face of modern violent Islamic extremism". He was held up as an example of how "the profile of the various groups who come under the rubric of the 'Indian Mujahideen', can be from any segment of society."[7] What happened since to the spectre of new educated professional as jihadi terrorist?

In 2008, Swami had made a shot at developing a kind of authoritative account of Indian jihadi groups outside of J & K, which he labels the 'well-tempered Jihad'. The paper was based largely on his own reportage, in turn based on 'highly placed sources' and investigators (and a nice game it is too, trying to untangle the references and citations of this burgeoning 'scholarship' on 'jihadi

---

5 *State v/s Shoaib Mirza @Chotu and Others*, Chargesheet filed by NIA, MHA, Govt of India. Copy on record.

6 *Countering Online Radicalisation: A Strategy for Action* by Tim Stevens and Peter Neumann, King's College London: International Centre for the Study of Radicalisation, 2009; "Jihadi Video and Auto-Radicalisation" by Maura Conway, *Lectures in Computer Science*, vol. 6376:108-118, 2008 and "Reality Bytes: Cyberterrorism and Terrorist 'Use' of the Internet", *First Monday* 7 (11), 2002.

7 "Spectre of the Educated Terrorist: Professionals are the new face of Terror as they swell the ranks of outfits like Indian Mujahideen" by Abhishek Bhalla, *The Daily Mail*, 02 September 2012. http://www.dailymail.co.uk/indiahome/indianews/article-2197303/Spectre-educated-terrorist-Professionals-new-face-terror-swell-ranks-outfits-like-Indian-Mujahideen.html#ixzz2Lvfva4xS

terror'). The key to understanding this well tempered jihad were the "three major strikes on mosques and Muslim civilians: at Malegaon in 2006, followed by the firebombing of a New Delhi-Lahore train and the Mecca Masjid in Hyderabad in 2007"... carried out by "Islamist terror groups".

> It is possible that the successive strikes on Muslim civilians ... were intended to educate: that is, to persuade followers that the restrictions imposed on the jihad in Jammu and Kashmir posed an existential threat to Islam and Pakistan. ... [And] Elaborately dressed as the Samjhauta Express attack to resemble an arson attack that could plausibly have been presented as the work of a Hindu fundamentalist mob, the bombing enabled [Hafeez] Saeed to represent it as part of 'a plot to massacre Muslims'.[8]

Hmmm.

So, is the current 'jihad' well tempered or not – given that none of these three incidents, so crucial to its tempering, turned out to be not the product of the jihadi groups? What of the elaborate plots, confidently narrated as the unfolding of the jihadi story in India, many of its twists and turns now established as its definitive signposts?

Anyhow, to return to the Bangalore case and sense of prejudice.

The author asks if it was "unreasonable" to hold the trio – Mirza, Siddiqui and Nalaband – on suspicion, considering that Mirza had access to sensitive information and Siddiqui visited various jihadist websites. (It is another matter that a journalist named Siddiqui visiting jihadist website raises suspicion, but one named Swami doesn't.) The NIA did, after all, release them when it found no prosecutable evidence against them.

---

8 "The Well-Tempered Jihad: the politics and practice of post-2002 Islamist terrorism in India" by Praveen Swami, *Contemporary South Asia*, 16:3, 2008, pp. 303-322.

They spent six months in jail, without a chargesheet being filed against them. Indeed, the Central Crime Branch (CCB) knew by September, less than a month after the arrest, and five months before the release, that they didn't have a case against Siddiqui. A statement, recorded by ACP KN Jithendranath of the CCB, on 20 September 2012 i.e., within 21 days of Siddiqui's arrest, shows that a vigorous examination of his email IDs had clearly established the absence of any connection between Siddiqui and the alleged terror conspiracy. It clearly states that the email ID of Muthi-ur-Rahman Siddiqui – which was checked in front of the panchas (witnesses) – contained "no incriminating materials/text/attachments".[9]

So, instead of showing gratitude to the police for having let them off without fabricating evidence or coercing confessions – as the author asks us to do – we should in fact be asking why they were kept in incarceration despite unambiguous proof of their innocence. Indeed, it needs to be remembered that the agencies took six months –180 days – to file the chargesheet, 90 days more than the normal period for filing charges under ordinary law. At the conclusion of the 90-day period, the CCB sought an extension, and received one instantly. Neither did it deem it fit to inform the court that they had no case against at least some of the arrested young men; nor did the court examine the merits or the progress of the investigation before granting a blanket extension for another 90 days for the chargesheet to be filed while the arrested continued to be in custody. It was a terror investigation. A matter of

---

9 "Muthiur Rehman was jailed despite proof of evidence" by Tariq Abdul Muhaimin, *Newzfirst.com*, 18 March 2013. http://www.newzfirst.com/web/guest/full-story/-/asset_publisher/Qd8l/content/muthi-ur-rahman-was-jailed-despite-proof-of-innocence?redirect=/web/guest/in%20focus

national security. Who dares question investigating agencies? Which court risks granting bail?

This, really, brings us to the characteristic nature of terror investigations and trials. It allows for cynical audits such as the one undertaken by Swami to dominate the mainstream discourse: So what, if three innocents were kept in custody for six months without bail. So what if their reputations were ground to dust; so what if they were denied the right to meet with their families long after their arrest: having to make do with furtive semi-secret meetings in parks and marriage halls granted by the CCB. And so what if they lost their jobs, their confidence, their peace of mind, condemned now to live for life with the harrowing memories. So what if people, total strangers, accost them on streets, and ask them, 'hey you, you are the one who was arrested by the police?' – something that makes them fearful of public places. It is just a bit of collateral damage. Too bad. But nothing to grieve over or complain about, really. Because this "has to be read against the possible harm to the community caused by the investigators' failure to arrest – which in this case, might have been several deaths."

It is not for nothing that a substantial portion of UAPA cases pertain not to actual events of violence, but to conspiracies. Conspiracies based on seizures of 'jihadi Urdu literature', SIMI magazines published before the ban on the organization, ID cards and membership forms of banned militant organisations, conveniently recovered from the pockets of 'operatives' of terror groups. Conspiracies which are described in minute detail in media commentary by security experts – much like Muthiur Rehman's online searches on jihadist websites – which build and sustain the guilt of accused and arrested 'terrorists'.

Yes, certainly, "police forces across the world are allowed, by law, to arrest suspects during investigation."

But there are norms and protocols laid down about the way in which these arrests may be made. The DK Basu Guidelines seem to be followed only in breach. How does incompetence or stretched resources justify the failure of the CCB to inform the parents of those arrested about their detention and arrests? Is it laziness which led the CCB to disallow parents to meet their arrested sons in custody?

And this is the most dangerous and perhaps the most enduring transformation yet wrought by anti-terror discourse: the presumption of guilt and the slow erosion of due process and rule of law; the urgency of national security providing justification for lowering of burden of proof, extended detention and denial of bail.

One of the cases discussed in our report was that of Lajpat Nagar blasts of 1996, in which the lower court had acquitted several accused while convicting others – handing death to three. Precisely two months after the report was released, the High Court acquitting two people serving on death row – and commuting the death sentence of the third into life imprisonment, noted that the trial court had convicted the three despite its own overt references to "lack of credibility of witnesses, in regard to circumstances, or general unreliability of prosecution". These, in the opinion of this court, pointed to a flawed understanding of "proof beyond reasonable doubt" in a criminal trial. The deficiencies are not reflective simply of inefficient investigation "but also throw up question marks as to the nature and truthfulness of the evidence produced". [10]

Shoddy investigation results partly from the belief that terrorism will serve as a sufficient alibi for evidence.

For all our author may protest, one of the touchstones of the discourse on terrorism is that its image of a terror-

---

10 *State versus Mohd. Naushad and Others*; Death Sentence Reference 2/2010, in the High Court of Delhi, pronounced on 22 November 2012. Copy on record.

ist is not an empty one, but one marked by signifiers of community. Don't go too far, just listen into what our top cops have to say:

> [I]n cases of terror attacks or communal riots, if the police goes after the perpetrators of the violence, and they happen to be mostly Muslim, you cannot, in the name of secularism, expect the police to act in proportion to their population. (Prakash Singh, former DG, BSF)[11]

> [T]here is nothing like Saffron terrorism. *It just doesn't exist in the Hindu pantheon.* (MN Singh, former Commissioner of Police, Mumbai)[12]

Since Swami picks on Mecca Masjid investigation as the prime example of the Liberal mis-assumption about police bias, let us spend a little time on it. He says:

> The claim that the police targeted Muslims for the Mecca Masjid bombing has been repeated so often as to become received truth. ... The truth is that 22 Muslim men were indeed arrested, and found innocent during trial. However, anyone who has taken the trouble to read First Information Report 198 filed at the Gopalapuram Police Station in 2007 knows not one of the arrests had anything to do with the Mecca Masjid case.
>
> Police officers driven by malice, or seeking to cover-up their incompetence, could have initiated false prosecutions linking these men to the Mecca Masjid attack. They did not – and went on to uncover the Hindutva terrorist network now blamed for the attack.

---

11 "Prison is the only place where Muslims are over-represented" by Seema Chishti, *Indian Express*, 28 October 2006. http://www.indianexpress.com/news/prison-is-the-only-place-where-muslims-are-overrepresented----------------/15622/0

12 http://www.ndtv.com/video/player/we-the-people/right-wing-terrorism-real-threat-or-overstated/265259?video-mostpopularEx-cop

Now the above is not simply a reproduction of IB dossiers, as the author is usually inclined to; it is worse. It is a deliberate and pernicious attempt to sanitize the Hyderabad police, its torture and its desperate efforts to implicate innocents in a terror conspiracy. Its almost fantastical, this timeline: 22 youths arrested, found innocent, released. Three cheers for our criminal justice system.

The fact is that around 70 youth were rounded up and taken to undisclosed, sometimes private, locations. Most of them from the Muslim-dominated inner city area of Moosaram Bagh. Some were picked up right after the Mecca Masjid blasts; others after the twin blasts three months later. They suffered varying periods of illegal detention and what many in the West euphemistically call 'enhanced interrogation techniques'. All of them were asked to confess to Mecca Masjid and Lumbini Park blasts in the city.

Here is an extract from the report of Advocate Ravi Chander Committee constituted by the Andhra Pradesh Minorities Commission after an outcry by the Muslim community of Hyderabad which felt besieged and hunted.

> Mohd. Abdul Raheem, Auto Driver, age 26 years, picked up on 3rd September 2007.
>
> 1. Arrested without being informed of charge
>
> 2. On September 3, about 4 police came home around 8 pm, and took me in an auto till Amberpet, thereafter taken in a two wheeler with eyes blindfolded.
>
> 3. Taken to Bolaram Police station, enquired till about midnight and the next morning taken, beaten, toes tied, beaten on foot of sole and abused (sic).
>
> 4. Became unconscious and as soon as I gained consciousness, there were about 7-8 others who were also beaten up.

Signs of torture were visible even in November when the Commission made its last visit to the Cheriapally jail.[13]

Advocate Ravi Chander concluded:

> It is clear that all victims belong to a single community and mostly to a single class. This may be insufficient to place the burden directly at a single doorstep, namely the police. They however surely tell a pattern. A seriously danger pattern.

Raheem was one of those booked under FIR number 198/2007 of Gopalapuram PS. Absolutely, do take the trouble of reading the FIR, as Swami suggests. It certainly does not breathe a word about Mecca Masjid blasts. But this is because the Hyderabad Police was not in charge of investigating the blasts by then. The case had already been transferred to the CBI. And the Hyderabad Police was chaffed to discover that the narco tests[14] and the confessions extracted from Raheem and others, didn't appeal to the CBI. So, what did it do? It created new cases of conspiracy: 198 and 75 of 2007. Both the cases ended in acquittal as the police could not bring absolutely anything on record to link these men with jihadi activities.[15]

Exactly what stage of literary evolution does Swami's 'liberal' play with facts and evidence belong to: "primitive fable" or "post-modern text"?

There is no denying the deep rot in the policing system, and that at least some of it has to do with it being un-

---

13 Investigation report submitted by L Ravi Chander, Advocate Commissioner for Minorities, copy on record.

14 "Kaleem Sings in Narco Test", TNN, 7th September 2007. http://articles.timesofindia.indiatimes.com/2007-09-07/hyderabad/27970584_1_mecca-masjid-blast-syed-imran-elder-brother

15 Copies of judgements (SC No. 544/207, in the Court of the VII Addl. Metropolitan Sessions Judge, Hyderabad, 31st December 2009 and SC number 42/2007, in the Court of the VII Addl. Metropolitan Sessions Judge, Hyderabad, 21 July 2008).

derstaffed, over worked, and being frugally paid. But this rot is also fundamentally about the impunity and power the police enjoys over ordinary citizens. The National Crime Records Bureau data for 2013 shows that 51,120 complaints were received against police personnel in that year, of which only 799 were eventually sent for trials or chargesheeted. A mere 1.5 per cent! About 8 per cent of complaints were referred for 'regular departmental action' – and the remaining were either dismissed as false or did not make it past departmental, magisterial or judicial enquiries.[16]

As for the comparison between rape and terrorism convictions, a sociological reading of the process of investigation and adjudication will tell us how different, indeed contrasting, are the results in the two situations – terrorism and rape – though both are framed by dominant social norms and prejudices. 'The woman was asking for it' is so deeply embedded in our moral universe that it is often the accused, and not the complainant (or the 'victim'), who is the subject of the system's sympathy and protection. On the other hand is the case of the one accused of terrorism. Lawyers have been attacked in court premises for daring to take up cases of the terror accused. They are tried under a law that doesn't favour bail and considerably dilutes the parametres of evidence.

To think that the malaise that afflicts the policing system in India in general is all that ails terror investigations ignores the fact that these investigations are conducted not by the local thana and the baton wielding constable but by elite, pampered forces such as the ATS and the Special Cell with unaccounted cash supplies, secret service funds and inexhaustible resources.

---

16 See Table 16-A, *Crime in India 2013*, National Crimes Record Bureau, Ministry of Home Affairs, p. 161.

Bias is not simply the bias of police and agencies. It isn't a bias that seeps in into the police force, unknown, unconsciously. Rather, it rests on the knowledge of that bias in our society, polity and media, and uses it to its full advantage. Prakash Singh and MN Singh know that they can get away with their jaundiced assumptions. It is for this reason that journalists can get away by projecting Muthiur Rehman Siddiqui as the new face of terror with no repercussion. It is for this reason that Swami can be blasé about his past blunders, about his predictions and projections of jihadi terror.

The thing with this bias is that it is not seen as a bias at all. It has been rendered as the commonsense.

Temples of Justice

The footwear was lined neatly outside the courtroom. Twelve men and two women crowded inside barefoot, waiting tensely for the judge to pronounce the verdict. Had this court condemned them already – forcing them to strip themselves off their chappals and sandals, as also a little bit of their dignity, each time they have had to enter this courtroom?

In mildly cold January of 2013, one of the most prominent trials in Madhya Pradesh has just wound down, after nearly five years. Crime number 256 was registered in the Kotwali police station of Khandwa in April 2006. Over the next two months, Khandwa police travelled around the country – to the neighbouring district of Burhanpur, to Kota in Rajasthan, to Azamgarh in Uttar Pradesh, returning to Indore and Jabalpur, scooping up suspects till they had 14 accused to show for their efforts. They were all charged under the draconian Unlawful Activities Prevention Act (UAPA) for "furthering the activities of the banned organization, SIMI". To prove their case, the police produced disclosures of the accused admitting their guilt, divulging details of where a cache of unlawful literature could be seized, and implicating their alleged comrades in these crimes. Sacks full of literature supposedly provided material evidence.

In the course of the trial it was brought to the attention of the court that the police had sealed none of the recoveries, a procedural requirement. The prosecution witnesses were hardly independent. One of them, Deepak (PW 1), admitted in court to being a member of the Bajrang Dal; another key witness Bajrang Lad (PW 6) had been booked in a criminal case (Cr. No. 737/04 dated 20.11.2004) in the same Kotwali thana. A third witness, Akash (PW 5) in his chief examination told the court that he had signed seizure memos under pressure from the police, and that in fact he had never accompanied the police party to Burhanpur where the three Siddiqi brothers were arrested and large hauls of unlawful material allegedly recovered from them. Precisely a year later, in a midnight raid, Akash was picked up by an officer posted in the Kotwali police station, illegally detained and tortured. Some months later, Akash committed suicide.

The material recoveries – unimpeachable evidence of the guilt of the accused – interestingly had been produced in different cases in Madhya Pradesh, and even Maharashtra. A receipt for contribution of Rs 500 ostensibly made by the accused Asiya towards the building fund of SIMI was submitted as part of evidence in another SIMI trial in Bhopal, *State vs Sajid Ali and Another* (FIR Number 302/2008), which ended in conviction. A banned orgnization would solicit funds for a building? And then record that transaction on a reciept? And the SIMI activist recording Asiya's contribution would enter her name as "Kumari" Asiya Khan?

Another alleged crucial piece of evidence against Asiya was a magazine called *Tehreek-e-Millat* recovered from her possession. In order to prove that the incriminating magazine belonged to her, the police pointed to her name written in her own hand across the coverpage. Now, seizure lists in four different cases investigated by Maharashtra ATS show up a curious item: *Tehreek-e-Millat Asiya*. Each of these have 'Asiya' written in the same handwriting.[1]

As we sat in the watery sunlight in the katcheri courtyard, half hopeful, half fearful of what was to come, even as bets were being wagered if the judgement would be pronounced that day or postponed – it was indeed postponed – the accused recalled the final arguments their lawyers had made. The infirmity of evidence, dubious seizures, doubtful witnesses, the fact that the magazines recovered were registered with Registrar of Newspapers of India (RNI), and never declared as 'unlawful' by any official notification, the inability of the prosecution to prove the handwriting of Asiya and Aquil Khilji on the contribution receipts; and so on it went, if only to confirm their own faith in the justness of the system that had so far offered them no deliverance.

"On what grounds could they be convicted under UAPA?" it was repeated like a refrain. And yet, convicted they were.

All but three were convicted under Sections 10 and 13 of the UAPA.[2] They were held guilty of being mem-

---

1 "2 Years, 5 Cities, 6 cases – and 'proof' everywhere is the same magazine" by Muzammil Jaleel, *Indian Express*, 1 October 2012. Among these cases were the Mumbai train blasts and the Malegaon blasts 2006.

2 Imran Ansari, Amanullah and Sarfaraz were acquitted of all charges. *State of Madhya Pradesh versus Mohd. Aquil Khilji* and Ohers, SC number 180/2006. Copy on record.

bers of an unlawful association and for committing an unlawful activity.

Stunningly, the court dismissed Akash's allegations of police pressure and chose to retain the initial part of his testimony where he had validated the prosecution story. His tragic story, reported widely in the local press, remained unobserved and uncommented by the court. The court did not find any credence in the defence argument that Bajrang Dal activist could be a motivated witness; neither did it feel that the witness who was booked in another crime in the same police station could be under the influence, or power, of the police.

In a baffling legal denouement, the court acquitted Asiya, Zafar, Khaleel and Shafeeque of the lighter charges of 153 A, 153 B and 295 A IPC, charges under which the burden of proof should be considerably lower than UAPA. None of the material allegedly recovered from these accused was found to "promote enmity between communities" or to make "assertions prejudicial to national integration", but the same material became the ground for their conviction for participation in unlawful activities.

Since 27 September 2001, when SIMI was declared a banned organization through a notification, Madhya Pradesh has seen an unrelenting registration of cases under UAPA throughout its major districts: 16 in Bhopal, of which 10 were booked between 27 September and 6 October 2001; 25 in Indore, of which 12 were booked in September-October 2001; 8 in Jabalpur, and a smattering of cases in Neemuch, Seoni, Guna, Khandwa, Dhar, Burhanpur and other places.[3]

---

3 These cases have been now compiled in the report, *Guilt By Association: UAPA Cases from Madhya Pradesh*, Jamia Teachers' Solidarity Association, New Delhi, 2013.

Reading the FIRs filed in the early days of the ban, one may assume that former members and office bearers of the organization were overcome by a sudden death wish. While their offices were being raided and sealed, and police and agencies conducting a 'crackdown' nationwide, SIMI activists and sympathizers appeared in public places, shouting slogans, waving pamphlets, pasting posters, exhorting others to join the newly banned organization, vowing to resist the ban on SIMI, and "provocating" – to use the MP police's favourite term – the Muslims against the government. And invariably, they were all apprehended in the middle of their unlawful activities and a rich haul of material seized from them. Never mind that these recoveries consisted of issues of SIMI's erstwhile mouthpiece, *Islamic Movement*,[4] copies of which surely would be in the possession of SIMI members on the evening of the declaration of the ban; posters inviting people to conferences long past; or simply literature in Urdu or Arabic. Somehow though this material could not be recovered from crowds listening to these unlawful orators, nor could anyone else be apprehended.

There is little to distinguish the FIRs filed in 2001 from the more recent ones, except that it appears that supplies of 'SIMI literature' have begun to wane, and we now see photocopies of *Islamic Movement*, SIMI receipts and other magazines beginning to make their appearance. FIR No. 184/2008 PS Khajrana for example tried to pass of photocopies of front and last page of an old copy of *Islamic Movement* as pamphlets._

Once booked in a crime under UAPA, every accused is fair game for further registration of crimes. This is the

---

4 Its publication was suspended after the ban in September 2001. So, all copies of the magazine predate the ban and its possession cannot constitute a crime. That, however, has not deterred the police from listing it as incriminating material.

method of the malicious madness that UAPA unleashes: a set of accused, booked in various permutations and combinations with identical crimes, similar situations – all recorded as if on boilerplate.

It is rare to find someone booked only in one case; 'case partners' abound everywhere. Imran Ansari, former state president of SIMI, acquitted in the Khandwa case, has spent over five years in prison in various jails, three of those in solitary confinement in Sagar. Just days before the ban on SIMI was declared, Imran travelled to Kanpur to help organize a SIMI conference. He was arrested and booked under Section 153. His five case partners were all local Kanpur boys. In December, in faraway Surat – while Imran was in jail – over a hundred men met to discuss minorities' educational rights, and were arrested in a midnight swoop by the police, which also claimed to have seized 'unlawful material' such as SIMI receipts. Imran was made an accused and in fact declared an absconder in this misnamed 'SIMI Surat Conference Case'.

Bizarre, however, is the normal in terror cases. In 2006, Imran was also charged with holding a "secret meeting" where a conspiracy to disturb the communal harmony and to perform terrorist acts in Indore was hatched. This secret meeting was conducted while Imran was being ferried by the police from Khandwa to Indore to be produced in court in connection with one of his numerous trials. The police claim that a witness revealed that Imran conferred with the owner of Wadi Chicken Centre, where the police party had stopped for a meal. Several others against whom FIRs had been registered in UAPA cases in different thanas had also participated in the meeting.

There is a unique osmotic quality to these UAPA cases, where guilt travels from one to another swiftly. There are cases, for example, where Imran may not be the accused, but the route to other accused. When arrested by the Khandwa police in crime number 256, Imran's 'disclosure' led to Sarfaraz in Jabalpur, from whom the police claimed to have seized a mobile phone. This phone was said to have been provided by none other than Imran, the Madhya Pradesh chief of SIMI, to further the activities of the unlawful association. On the basis of this mobile phone – which, as it turned out, was registered neither in the name of Imran, nor of Sarfaraz, but of one Ram Prasad from Ujjain – Sarfaraz was pulled into the Khandwa case while a separate case (Crime No. 706/06, PS Gohalpur) was registered in Jabalpur. The same mobile phone with the same phone number was shown as seizure in two different cases in two different cities. Sarfaraz was tried twice for the same allegation of possessing a mobile phone used in perpetuating unlawful acts. For five years, he continued to petition the High Court seeking discharge in the Jabalpur case but received no relief. He was granted bail by the Jabalpur High Court only after he had spent one and a half years in Khandwa jail. In the Jabalpur case, he was finally convicted under Section 153 but acquitted of UAPA charges.

But there is something even graver. Sarfaraz was consistently denied bail by the trial court in Khandwa despite the fact that government sanction to prosecute him under UAPA had not been secured – indeed it was not received even till the conclusion of the trial, a fact which resulted in his acquittal. His entire trial had been patently illegal – as had been his incarceration.

As terror trials go, *State versus Aquil Khilji* was unexceptional, both in the manner of investigation, prosecution and its conclusion. Often, convictions have been handed out on the basis of police witnesses and recoveries alone, disregarding the fact of rampant violation of procedural norms by the police, by overlooking the fact that incriminating literature predates the ban on the organization, by refusing to weigh evidence at each step, by ignoring the most obvious lack of sanction from the authorities, by turning a blind eye to the frivolity of prosecution case to allow framing of charges under such serious sections.

In *State versus Irfan* (FIR No. 251/01, PS Gwaltoli, Indore), for example, the only two independent witnesses – Chandar and Rajesh – thoroughly denied the police story. An expert witness testified that the Urdu literature seized contained nothing against the State or society, and in fact only consisted of veneration of God. Lack of evidence though appeared hardly to be of any significance to the court, which convicted him under Section 10 of UAPA.

Then there is the famous Pithampur case of Dhar (FIR No. 120/2008). It triggered a chain reaction across the state, leading to the registration of 18 UAPA cases within one month, and another four over next six months. The modus operandi of registering false cases was revealed rather unwittingly by the IO of the Pithampur case, BPS Parihar in the SIMI Tribunal of 2010. He placed before the Tribunal copies of 18 identical letters, all dated 29 March 2008, written by Chanchal Shekhar, SP of Dhar to his colleagues in 18 districts of Madhya Pradesh, providing them a list of names and telephone numbers recovered from the 13 SIMI office bearers and members arrested in the Pithampur case. The letters urged the respective SPs to "examine the information pertaining to your district and send information about the said persons with SIMI and also take action against them at your level." Reference has been made to this letter in several of these 18 cases.[5]

The Pithampur case itself was based on recoveries of literature. The court turned down the argument put forth

5 Affidavit filed by BPS Parihar (PW 58) in UAPA Tribunal 2010. Copy on record.

by the lawyer for two of the accused from whose farmhouse the offensive recoveries had allegedly been made, that that there was no evidence to prove their culpability in any unlawful activity. True, said the Court, nothing documentary has been placed before it to prove their guilt. "However, this does not have an adverse impact [for the prosecution's case] because it is not usually possible to find such proof; one cannot in fact expect or desire formal proof."

These are the temples of justice in Madhya Pradesh. Leave your footwear outside.

Truth is Stranger than Fiction

"Truth is stranger than fiction", wrote the division bench of the Gujarat High Court in 2010.[1] The High Court had invoked Mark Twain to explain the two letters recovered in perfect, unsoiled condition from the bullet-perforated and blood-soaked bodies of two fidayeens. It then confirmed the convictions to the six men – including life imprisonment and death sentences to three – handed out by the POTA Special Court of Ahmedabad.

In September 2002, a deadly attack on the Akshardham temple in Gandhinagar left over 30 dead and scores injured. The NSG, requisitioned from Delhi, finally shot dead the two-armed raiders after hours long gun battle. A complaint was lodged the same day. For almost one year, the investigations meandered and changed hands from the

1 *State vs Adambhai*, Criminal Confirmation Case Number 2 of 2006 with Cr Appeal Number 1675 of 2006 with Cr Appeal Number 1328 of 2006, Gujarat High Court, Judges: R.M. Doshit and K.M. Thaker, 1 June 2010.

local police, to the ATS, finally reaching the crime branch on the evening of 28 August 2003.

At 6.30 pm, GL Singhal assumed charge of the investigation. At 8 pm, he recorded the statement of the first prosecution witness (PW 50) on the information provided by DIG DG Vanzara. The following day, on 29 August, accused numbers 1 - 5 were arrested. Provisions of POTA, which had been absent in the original complaint and FIR were added on 30 August. On 31 August, the IGP Operations ATS Gujarat received a fax message from IGP Kashmir stating that one Chand Khan in their custody had confessed to his involvement in the Akshardham attack. Though Chand Khan's – and the Jammu and Kashmir police's – story contradicted the Gujarat ATS' in that he claimed to be working for Lashkar with no local support, a few days in ATS custody were enough to iron out all discrepencies and discordant notes.[2]

It turned out that the Urdu handwriting on the letters recovered from the dead fidayeens matched that of accused number 4. Moreover, the six accused readily agreed to make confessional statements detailing their roles in the conspiracy, first before the SP Sanjay Gadhvi (PW 78) and then before the chief judicial magistrate (PW 99). Meanwhile, an ambassador car was recovered from the accused number 6 from Jammu and Kashmir. This was the car allegedly used to ferry the fidayeens from Kashmir to Ahmedabad via Bareilly.

All loose ends taken care of and neatly tied up. What was there not to believe in the prosecution story? The Special POTA Court passed its judgement convicting all six in July 2006. In June 2010, the High Court opined that

---

2 See *The State, Democracy and Anti-Terror Laws in India* by Ujjwal Kumar Singh, Sage, Delhi, 2007, pp. 177-80.

the "the offence of criminal conspiracy of mass killing of Hindus in Gujarat; of promoting enmity between the two groups on ground of religion; of inviting support for a terrorist organization; of arranging and managing meeting/s to support a terrorist organization; of inviting another to provide money, of receiving money and of providing money for the purpose of terrorism; of use of prohibited arms and explosives; of terrorist act of mass killing without provocation; of attempt to murder and of abetment are established."

The real story of the Akshardham case is not in the malicious investigation, which is by now rather familiar. Even the cast is well known: GL Singhal, DG Vanzara and their cronies in ATS and Crime Branch. Reading judgements and chargesheets of terror cases induces a sense of ennui, like watching a series of mind numbing B-grade potboilers, where the plot, camera angles, dialogues, all resemble each other to the extent that they all segue into one mess, difficult to extricate one from another. For example, the fortuitous discovery of fragments of papers that point the investigators straight to the accused. In the Red Fort attack case (2000) a paper slip bearing a telephone number was said to have fallen from the pocket of an escaping terrorist, nailing the main accused Md. Arif @ Ashfaq. In the Parliament attack case (2001), telephone numbers recovered from the dead terrorists led to Mohammad Afzal, Shaukat Husain Guru, Afsan Guru and SAR Geelani. Then there are hazy lines which join SOG (special operations group) in Kashmir to the investigative agencies in Delhi or Gujarat. Also characteristic is the efficiency of investigating agencies – the ATS, or the Special Cell, or the Crime Branch – that are able to crack cases, arrest accused, and wrap up confessions in no time.

The real story, however, lies in what happened in the courts and the judicial offices. On 16 May 2014, the Supreme Court in acquitting five of the six convicted men who had appealed against their conviction liberally used the terms "perverse", "injustice", "manifestly unreasonable", "a gross violation of fundamental rights and basic human rights" to refer to the previous judgements and its power to overturn those.[3] So deeply troubled was the apex court by the business of the POTA Special Court and the High Court, which had heard this case that it also acquitted accused number 1, who had not even appealed before it. Calling what played out in the courts merely judicial abdication would be too polite. It was nothing short of absolute abnegation of judicial responsibility.

For the long list of crimes the six accused in the Akshardham attack were charged with, and the severe penalties imposed upon them, the evidence produced was shockingly sparse. The bulk of the evidence were the five confessions extracted from the accused (accused number 5 had refused to confess) under Section 32 of POTA.

Remember, POTA allowed the admission of confession made to a police officer – otherwise inadmissible under the Indian Evidence Act – as evidence to be used against the accused. Nonetheless, the Supreme Court laid down several safeguards to ensure that the confessions were free and voluntary.[4] These included the issuance of

---

3 *Adambhai Sulemanbhai Ajmeri & Others versus State of Gujarat*, Criminal Appeals Numbers 2295-2296 of 2010 with Criminal Appeal Number 45 of 2011, Supreme Court of India, Judge: V. Gopala Gowda, 16 May 2014.

4 Subsection 1 of Section 32 allowed for admission of a confession made before a police officer not lower in rank than a Superintendent of Police as evidence. Subsections 2-5 contained the safeguards, namely that the person making the confession should be explained in writing that the confession can be used against him; the confession be recorded in an atmosphere free from threat or inducement; the maker of the confession should be produced before a Chief Judicial Magistrate within 48 hours; the CJM has

letters of caution to the accused. Such letters of caution should precede the confession, and should in fact form one seamless document. The confessions in this case, recorded by DCP Sanjay Gadhvi, stand apart from the letters of caution he is said to have issued to the accused when they were produced before him by the Crime Branch for the recording of confession. Moreover, in his cross- examination, Gadhvi admitted that he had not bothered to examine the accused to reassure himself that accused had not been tortured or physically assaulted. Neither did he – he said in the course of the cross examination – assure the accused persons that not making the confessional would not endanger them. The Supreme Court thought it fit to reproduce an extract from his intimation letter to demonstrate the casual manner in which 'procedure' was followed. Gadhvi's letter read:

> "...your statement under section 32 of the POTA before the Superintendent of Police is to be taken. But you are not bound to make this statement or confession and the confession that you will make could be used against you as evidence. So it is informed to you that you give this statement willingly and free from any kind of pressure or threat or allurement."

To these men, who had been in the custody of the Crime Branch for a month, Gadhvi gave a mere 15 minutes to reflect over their decision to confess. But if one could try and understand Gadhvi's desire to side with his fellow police officers, who had brought the accused before him for the recording of confession – how does one excuse the chief judicial magistrate, before whom the accused were presented to fulfill the requirement under

---

to verify the voluntariness of the confession and the well being of the person making the confession.

32(4) of POTA? This provision required the magistrate to test the voluntariness of the confession.

First, the rapidity with which the CJM enquired about the wellbeing of the accused, recorded the statement, read it back to the accused and signed it, could have given Singhal himself an inferiority complex. Accused number 4's statement, for instance, which ran into 15 pages, was recorded, read out, and procedure followed in a flat 30 minutes. The CJM admitted during cross examination that he had not made "inquiry with any police officers with regard to the said confessions. I had not asked the two accused produced before me as to whether they need any lawyer or not. I had not taken the said accused persons in my custody."

But what vitiated the safeguards entirely was the CJM's direction to return the accused to the custody of the crime branch rather than to judicial custody. Imagine this: a man in custody of the crime branch for a month; produced before a senior police officer who neither cares to check if force has been applied on him to confess, nor reassures him that he wouldn't be returned on remand to the crime branch, records his confessional statement; within 48 hours, the accused is produced before a magistrate, who repeats the callousness of the police officer before him. The man is returned to the investigating agency. Would this confession be deemed as fair, voluntary and hence admissible incriminating evidence against the accused?

Both the POTA Court and the Gujarat High Court found confessions recorded when the accused were under the absolute power of the crime branch to be admissible. Both agreed that the prosecution had proved that procedure had been followed. Both concurred, in contravention to settled principle, that Section 32 (5) of POTA did not compel the CJM recording the statement to send the accused to judicial custody – not unless torture was expressly alleged. Both paid little heed to the disappearance of medical records of the accused, which could have proved the allegation of fracture resulting from torture. Both dismissed retractions of confessions, wherein the accused alleged brutal violence, which had forced them to confess, as mechanical and tutored.

Neither was exercised by the fact that the case unraveled with such great speed as soon as the crime branch took over the investigations. The precipitous speed of investigation was referred to by the HC indulgently as "gathering of momentum". Neither cared that DG Vanzara, whose role in pointing towards the PW 50 triggered the other arrests, was not listed as a witness, depriving the defence the right to cross-examine him. Neither saw that the state Home Ministry had granted the sanction for POTA swiftly with little regard to facts and without application of mind.

It did not trouble either the POTA Court or the High Court that there was in fact not a shred of evidence save for these dubious confessions that could link the accused to the crime. There were of course the letters, retrieved in pristine condition from the slain militants. That the handwriting expert who proved A-4's handwriting on the recovered letters could not read or write Urdu, or even differentiate between Urdu, Persian or Arabic, was a trifle neither court could be bothered with. The only 'proof' offered for hawala transactions, a diary with entries of cash under the code name 'Jihad', was accepted without a trace of irony. The ambassador car driven by accused number 6 had been seized from the compound of the SOG in Srinagar, and no papers existed to demonstrate that the car belonged to him – or had indeed been recovered from him.

In the end, what one is left with, are the contradictory confessions, which both courts found adequate to sentence three men to death.

The application of POTA thus was crucial to the sustenance of the case.

The trial records of the Akshardham case validate the fears expressed by civil liberties activists. PUCL had argued before the Supreme Court against allowing police officers to record confessions, cautioning that once the police had obtained confessions, the magistrates would only be used mechanically to put the seal of approval. It is evident here that safeguards remained a lifeless formality, hardly ever held up to any reasonable scrutiny.

The Akshardham attack case mirrors the Parliament attack case in more ways than one: from the manner of investigation, the weak evidence, to the rampant flouting of safeguards, to the arguments in court defending all this. 'Collective conscience' ultimately outweighed the respect for substantive procedure in the latter. Adam Ajmeri, accused number 2 in Akshardham, was saved Afzal Guru's fate by the Supreme Court. But can we offer that as consolation to a man who lost eleven years of his life?

The Supreme Court in writing the judgement in the present case is keenly conscious of the sordid history of this law.

> POTA was repealed in 2004. Yet, the trials, its implementation has entailed, are continuing till date. POTA was repealed for the gross violation of human rights it caused to the accused persons due to abuse of power by the police. This is an important aspect to be kept in mind while deciding this case and hence, it was pertinent to mention this in the beginning to say that we are wary of the abuse the provisions of this Act might bring.

POTA was repealed in 2004 when the last NDA government was ousted. In its place, the pre-existing Unlawful Activities Prevention Act was fortified. Though UAPA does not allow confessions as evidence, as much as a whisper of the word 'terrorism' can produce some wonders. The sessions court, convicting Arif in the Red Fort attack case held that: "Even *if* there is some torture or illegality committed by the police officials in the course of investigation, the same does not render the evidence inadmissible."[5]

Terror cases are tried under UAPA for years without sanction being obtained; and when granted, sanction is often proved in court by way of a lowly clerk in the state home ministry testifying to his officer's signature on the sanction order. When the UAPA was being amended in the Parliament following the 2008 Mumbai attack, LK Advani had rued the absence of admissibility of confessions. Today, when his former protégé, who built his initial political career at least partly on the blusterous rhetoric of terrorism – deploying Godhra, Akshardham, Haren Pandya murder and the numerous other POTA cases and encounter killings as strategic political resources – is in power, prepare for a new counterterrorism regime.

As though to inaugurate it, GL Singhal, arrested in 2013 by the CBI for leading the Ishrat Jahan fake encounter, and protagonist of the Akshardham attack case, has been reinstated by the Gujarat government.

---

5 See *An Unfair Verdict: A Report on the Red Fort Attack*, Peoples' Union for Democratic Rights, Delhi, 2006.

Part III

The Security Metaphysic

The Security Metaphysic

Section I

"If it's a good man, he will be stopped by the pneumatic tyre killers." The chief operating officer explains earnestly, pointing to the mean looking metallic teeth that threaten to slash to ribbons anything that rolls over it. "If it's a bad man however, he will continue on. Then these bollards will rise and stop him." As he says this, a metallic cylinder rises from the floor with great sound and fury. And just in case the 'bad man' escapes this too, there is the crash rated barrier. A large screen runs an animation video on spool, graphically demonstrating how the tyre killers, bollards and barriers can combat an onslaught of suicide bombers. Together, these three are the core of the "affordable and impregnable security from Israel" being showcased at the Homeland Security Fair in Greater Noida. A 100 per cent owned subsidiary of a Holon-based company that offers "perimeter protection solutions" – a popular phrase in this market – these makers of tyre killers and bollards set up shop in Ahmedabad in 2010.

"Why Ahmedabad?"

"Its closer to the port and there are no workers unions in Ahmedabad." He smiles, the wry smile of those who feel entitled to labour trouble-free factories. It is also a smile that expects empathy in return. He gets none.

"So, is business good?"

"Between 2010 and now [2012], we have already secured Grand Chola and Bombay Stock Exchange."

A more recent visit to their website informs that they have also bagged orders for bollards at Hyatt chain of hotels, for an equity fund office in Madhya Pradesh and Tata Motors in Jamshedpur. Business is good. No doubt on that count. The COO, himself a major in the Indian Army went to Israel to attend a course on suicide attacks and swiftly decided on an early retirement in favour of this lucrative security business. Indeed, this industry is swarming with ex-army men, short service commission officers having finished their terms, voluntary retirees and venerable generals and major generals. Some, senior managers and directors; some, spokespersons and consultants; some, editors of trade magazines; and others simply 'security experts' and regular fixtures on TV shows.

The cavernous interiors of the Noida Expo building are filled with companies – British, Israeli, Korean, Taiwanese and Indian multinationals such as Godrej to down-right local, cottage types operating out of West Delhi – peddling a plethora of wares. Bollards are a favourite of course, tyre killers and biometric technology are hot too – but the winner hands down is the CCTV camera. There is a great array to choose from: intelligent video armonia (because a large number of cameras must be able to work together "like musicians in an orchestra"), "full High Definition network solution" and "State of the art surveillance". And oh, we have a heart: part of the proceeds from the sales of Ever Focus – offering "total surveillance solutions" – go to the NGO CRY (Child Rights and You).

The hard-sell can produce an unintended irony though. The Japanese Fujitsu advertises PalmSecure, allegedly "the world's most advanced biometric authentication system", as "the fastest, simplest, most versatile and efficient system available to verify your identity: *to make sure that you are, in fact, who you say you are*." Who precisely is it targeting? Those very, whose identity is to be authenticated through its technology? Or perhaps, it imagines a world where we are all willing subjects and pliant bodies, participating in our own surveillance and monitoring.

The Homeland Security Fair is only one of the many exhibitions and expos that focus on the sale of surveillance devices, protective (as in "perimeter protection") equipment and associated ancillaries. It is, in fact, a rather latecomer in the field.

The first mover was the Ministry of Defence, which set up the Defence Exhibition Organisation as early as 1981 to showcase the indigenous defence industry, entirely public sector with DRDO and ordnance factories, by organizing exhibitions in India and abroad. Beginning with Aero India in 1996, and the Land and Naval Systems exhibition, Defexpo, in 1999,[1] its biennale exhibitions rapidly established themselves as preeminent trade hubs, so much so that by 2010, the total area of exhibition had spread to 40,000 square metres – from 17000 sq metres in the 2008 exhibition – and the rental had skyrocketed. Israel led the foreign exhibitors in renting as much as 1200 square metres of display space by shelling out Rs 3.5

1 Ministry of Defence, Government of India. http://mod.nic.in/product%26supp/

crores.[2] By 2012, it had grown even bigger: 567 exhibitors from 32 countries: SAAB, ABG Shipyard, Boeing, Polaris, HAL, Mahindra and Mahindra, TATA, Sirkosky, shipbuilders Navantia, Israel Aerospace Industry, Vectra, BAE Systems.[3]

What draws these builders of ships, makers of helicopters, manufacturers of airplanes and assorted military vehicles to the India expo in such large numbers? Inaugurating the Expo, the then-Minister of State for Defence, Pallam Raju, appreciated the "unprecedented growth" of the Defexpo, which he saw as a reflection of the "size of the defence market in India".[4]

To be sure, these are not empty words of a minister seducing investors. Budgetary allocations for defence have been steadily soaring the past few years. In 2011-12, the Union Defence Budget comprised 1.8 per cent of the total GDP; in the following year, the budget shot up marginally to 1.9 per cent of the GDP.

The 15-year Long Term Integrated Perspective Plan (LTIPP) approved by the Defence Acquisition Council, which is the source of defence planning, envisages the allocation of defence to touch three per cent of the total GDP – a feat yet not attained.[5]

However, in absolute numbers, the outlays for defence far outstrip allocations for social welfare programmes. Its share in terms of expenditure was higher than the combined spending of health and family welfare, school education and literacy schemes, higher education and rural welfare. (See table)[6]

---

2 http://ajaishukla.blogspot.in/2010/02/special-coverage-of-defexpo-2010.html

3 http://www.youtube.com/watch?v=ziK54V_uuZM

4 http://www.youtube.com/watch?v=3MHy4zo_fCc

5 http://www.idsa.in/idsacomments/DefenceBudget2013-14_acowshish_080313

6 Tables courtesy Rajeev Kumar.

Expenditure by Departments (Rs. Crores)							
	Actual	*Actual*	*Actual*	*Actual*	*Actual*	*Revised*	*Budget*
	2007-2008	*2008-2009*	*2009-2010*	*2010-2011*	*2011-2012*	*2012-2013*	*2013-2014*
Defence Total	108550.60	136556.18	180018.34	194605.80	213673.28	223003.52	253345.91
Health and Family Welfare	13951.00	16505.95	19554.09	22764.5	24355.08	25927.00	33278.00
School Education and Literacy	20942.69	24370.91	24466.07	36432.5	40641.35	45542.00	52701.00
Higher Education	6242.25	11206.58	13963.33	15471.79	19505.07	21277.00	26750.00
Rural Development	28816.73	56881.18	56637.11	72109.37	64263.46	52044.83	74477.65
Grand Total	712671.21	883956.00	1024487.46	1197327.73	1304364.98	1430825.24	1665297.32

Growth in Expenditure by Departments (%)

	Actual	*Actual*	*Actual*	*Actual*	*Actual*	*Revised*	*Budget*
	2007-2008	*2008-2009*	*2009-2010*	*2010-2011*	*2011-2012*	*2012-2013*	*2013-2014*
Defence Total		25.80	31.83	8.10	9.80	4.37	13.61
Health and Family Welfare		18.31	18.47	16.42	6.99	6.45	28.35
School Education and Literacy		16.37	0.39	48.91	11.55	12.06	15.72
Higher Education		79.53	24.60	10.80	26.07	9.08	25.72
Rural Development		97.39	-0.43	27.32	-10.88	-19.01	43.10
Grand Total		24.03	15.90	16.87	8.94	9.70	16.39

Share of Departments in total Expenditure (%)

	Actual	*Actual*	*Actual*	*Actual*	*Actual*	*Revised*	*Budget*
	2007-2008	*2008-2009*	*2009-2010*	*2010-2011*	*2011-2012*	*2012-2013*	*2013-2014*
Defence Total	15.23	15.45	17.57	16.25	16.38	15.59	15.21
Health and Family Welfare	1.96	1.87	1.91	1.90	1.87	1.81	2.00
School Education and Literacy	2.94	2.76	2.39	3.04	3.12	3.18	3.16
Higher Education	0.88	1.27	1.36	1.29	1.50	1.49	1.61
Rural Development	4.04	6.43	5.53	6.02	4.93	3.64	4.47

These high figures for defence spending weren't high enough for some though. Defence budget watchers complained that the forces had underspent the outlays allocated to them in 2011-12, surrendering a portion at the time of revised estimates.[7] A *Times of India* report sensationalized and hyped the alleged cuts in capital outlays by as much as Rs. 100 crores, which, it predicted would stymie the acquisition process.[8] This was despite the fact that 2013-14 budget had displayed an increase in both revenue and capital expenditure – despite the Defence Minister's warning that a dip in budget was in the offing, the finance minister had refrained from slashing the defence funds. Indeed, the outlays had bloated, except that the percentage of GDP had dropped to 1.79 as opposed to previous year's healthy 1.93.[9]

India has been for some years now in the throes of a procurement cycle. As its Soviet-era jets and submarines begin to age and rust, and as it is blinded by its own pretensions to regional hegemony, its multitudinous insurgencies calling to be quelled, and as the state-owned ordnance factories and PSUs fail to match up – the wheels of the procurement cycle turn, slowly, laboriously, oiled along by DPP. Defence Procurement Procedure, formulated in 2001, has undergone several revisions, each amendment further aiding private participation, turning private players from mere suppliers of raw materials and parts to full-scale licensed producers.

In early 2014, SIPRI released 2009-2013 figures of international transfer of weapons, which confirmed India

---

7 http://www.idsa.in/idsacomments/IndiasDefenceBudget2012-13_LaxmanBehera_200312

8 "Rs 10,000 crore cut in defence budget hits critical procurement deals" by Rajat Pandit, *Times of India*, 6 February 2013.

9 http://www.idsa.in/idsacomments/IndiasDefenceBudget_balachandran_040313

at top of the pile.[10] India accounted for 14 per cent of global arms imports, and its imports were three times greater than either China or Pakistan.[11] Its preeminence derived from its extensive shopping through the 2000s, reflected in the budgetary spends: over 100 Su-30MKI combat aircraft from Russia, three A-50EhI airborne early warning aircrafts (with components sourced from Israel, Russia and Uzbekistan), an Akula nuclear-powered submarine from Russia;[12] the first of eight P-8I anti-submarine warfare aircraft, ten C 17 Globemaster III Airlifters and six C 130 J Super Hercules Transport aircraft from the United States;[13] six Scorpene submarines from France.[14] The Defence Minister announced in the Lok Sabha in May 2013 that the procurement of 100 self-propelled artillery howitzers was on the anvil.[15]

But the most massive deal ever in the military history of the country, and one of the biggest in the world too, produced by Indian Air Force's modernization drive is the purchase of 126 Medium multi role combat aircraft worth

---

10 http://www.sipri.org/media/pressreleases/2014/AT_march_2014

11 http://books.sipri.org/files/FS/SIPRIFS1403.pdf

12 http://articles.timesofindia.indiatimes.com/2013-03-19/india/37842789_1_major-conventional-weapons-arms-exports-arms-imports

13 http://pib.nic.in/newsite/erelease.aspx?relid=78432

14 "Much in Demand" by Kalyani Datta, *Gfilesindia.com*; Access at http://www.gfilesindia.com/frmArticleDetails.aspx?id=224&Name=DEFENCE%20-%20def%20expo%20 2012

15 "Army to procure artillery howitzers, 3 Indian vendors selected", *Economic Times*, 6 May 2013. http://articles.economictimes.indiatimes.com/2013-05-06/news/39065496_1_defence-minister-scorpene-project-defence-sector

upwards of 15 billion USD.[16] There is some dispute as to what the real costs of the purchase will ultimately be, with some arguing that it should have been estimated at USD 27 billion even in 2009.[17]

Military expenditure in India is forecasted to grow at a compound annual growth rate of 8.3 per cent and is expected to exceed $ 75 billion per year by 2020.[18] Different agencies estimated slightly different numbers for the future defence budgets but all converged on the prediction that it was only bound to grow. As the brochure from one of the many defence exhibitions cheerfully outlined: "The Indian government has indicated no slowdown in homeland security and defence spending despite the global meltdown."

A recession-struck Western arms industry looks at India's insatiable appetite for arms and defence equipment to stay afloat. All the big boys of international arms trade have come out to play in India.

Section II

In 1961, when demitting office, the US President Dwight D. Eisenhower warned of the absolute influence – "economic, political, even spiritual" – which "the conjunction of an immense military establishment and a large arms industry" wielded, and which could be "felt in every city,

---

16 "MMRCA deal likely by April: IAF Chief", *The Hindu*, 21 September 2012. http://www.thehindu.com/news/national/mmrca-deal-likely-by-april-iaf-chief/article3919363.ece

17 http://www.defenseindustrydaily.com/mirage-2000s-withdrawn-as-indias-mrca-fighter-competition-changes-01989/ and http://web.archive.org/web/20140222022509/http://www.dnaindia.com/india/report-dna-exclusive-100-price-escalation-on-rafale-fighter-aircraft-to-rs-175-lakh-crore-likely-to-dent-iaf-s-strike-capability-1957107

18 https://www.frost.com/sublib/display-market-insight.do?id=256530829

every State house, every office of the Federal government." He urged his successor and the American citizens to "guard against the acquisition of unwarranted influence, whether sought or unsought, by the military industrial complex. The potential for the disastrous rise of misplaced power exists and will persist."[19]

But it is precisely this caution that our commentators, defence analysts and security experts are urging the government to cast away, and instead to embrace the 'military industrial complex'.

The ripples of the New Economic Policy reached the last bastion of the public sector – defence – only in 2001, when the newly minted DPP allowed 100 per cent participation by the private sector with foreign direct investment (FDI) permissible up to 26 per cent, subject to security clearances and licensing. The DPP of 2006 introduced the offset policy requiring all foreign vendors who were making sales upwards of Rs 300 crores to spend 30 per cent of their costs in India either through direct purchase of defence products and components manufactured by either the Defence PSUs or private defence industry; FDI in Indian defence industries for joint ventures, co-production agreements etc and finally FDI in defence R & D. Defence Offset Facilitation Agency (DOFA) was set up to "assist potential vendors in interfacing with the Indian defence industry for identifying potential offset products/projects as well as provide requisite data and information for this purpose."[20] The list of products which could be used by foreign vendors to discharge their offsets obligations has since then been expanding: from 13 products identified in 2008, the DPP now includes 27 products with the express

---

19 http://coursesa.matrix.msu.edu/~hst306/documents/indust.html

20 http://mod.nic.in/dofa.htm

addition of "Products for Internal Security" and "Civil Aerospace Products".

Traditional players like Tatas and Mahindra were quick to adapt to this windfall. Anand Mahindra claimed in an interview at the Def Expo 2012 that Mahindra had smelt the opportunity a decade earlier – just when the procurement wheel was about to turn – and had presciently engineered a shift in their approach to the defence market in setting up Mahindra Defence Systems and Mahindra Aerospace. From its earlier approach of "here is a truck, lets paint it olive green and turn it into a military vehicle", it has moved to "strategically, what's the path forward? What are the defence requirements of this country? In which areas? Where can we build advantages?" But lest he overplay the defence opportunity and 'strategic importance' of his company's move, he adds quickly, "in fact it is a need more than an opportunity".[21]

So even as one witnesses the surge in foreign arms companies fishing for contracts in India, Indian private sector – even that traditionally not involved in defence sector – realizing the spoils to be had from the offset policy is increasingly venturing into defence to cash in on the offsets policy.

Reliance India Limited (RIL), India's biggest private sector company, which built its riches on textiles and polyester, before expanding into fibre intermediates, plastics, petrochemicals, and then oil and gas explorations, announced its entry into the defence market by hiring Boeing's head in India, and then signing a deal with his former employers to partner in its offsets requirements in its project to supply P8I naval reconnaissance aircraft to the Indian Navy. A "more definitive agreement" is also in

---

21 Interview with Anand Mahindra: The Car and Bike Show on NDTV Profit. See full video here: http://www.youtube.com/watch?v=_fTZcYxGUiw

the offing. Its application with Department of Industrial Planning and Policy (DIPP) sought an industrial license to "design, develop, manufacture, equipment and components, including airframe, engines, radars, avionics and accessories for military and civilian aircraft, helicopters, unmanned airborne vehicles and aerostats". RIL has indicated to the press its intention of pumping in $1 billion and hiring between 1500 - 2000 engineers in the near future in its aerospace division. This only demonstrates the expectations of high growth the market leaders have from this sector.[22]

From purveyors of tea to makers of medicines, the defence sector allures and beckons all. In 2011, Rossell Tea Ltd metamorphosed into Rossell India Limited to more accurately reflect its new interests in the aerospace and defence segments, soon tying up with the Canadian firm CAE Canada "to provide simulation training solutions to the Indian defence market".[23]

When the pharma giant Piramal was looking to foray into new sectors, defence and security solutions was one of its chosen fields, hiring retired Deputy Chief of Air Staff, Air Marshal Nirdosh Tyagi, whose experience in procurement and production would "come in handy".[24]

---

22 "RIL lines up close to $1 billion plan in aerospace sector, may hire around 1,500 people" by Ullekh NP, *Economic Times*, 28 July 2012. http://articles.economictimes.indiatimes.com/2012-07-28/news/32906758_1_ril-lines-reliance-security-solutions-global-hub; and "Will Mukesh Ambani's defence Aerospace gambit pay off for RIL" by Ullekh NP, *Economic Times*, 12 May 2013.

http://economictimes.indiatimes.com/articleshow/20007427.cms

23 http://www.rossellindia.com/ and "Rossell India Ties up with Canadian Firm in Defence Sector" *The Hindu*, 10 August 2012. http://www.thehindubusinessline.com/companies/rossell-india-ties-up-with-canadian-firm-in-defence-sector/article3750501.ece

24 "Ajay Piramal ropes in family, friends; to foray into home security solutions, defence and drug discovery" by M. Sabarinath,

The same year, Piramal Enterprises acquired a 27.83 stake in Israeli Bluebird Aero Systems, manufacturer of Unmanned Aerial Systems, for Rs 40 crore. Reports circulating in the media suggested that Piramal group was wooing the US-based Global Technical Systems, which has produced AN/APS-151 Radar, an airborne surveillance tool that can be installed on unmanned aerial vehicles.[25] In less than a year from its launch, Piramal systems had signed a MOU with the Swedish group Saab to produce land electronic defence systems (LEDS).[26]

The country currently imports about 70 per cent of its defence equipment. Much handwringing has been done in security circles on this dependence on fickle international traders. The need for indigenization has been underscored often enough. While announcing finalization of the new DPrP in end-2010, Defence Minister A K Antony declared that the DPrP had become necessary because "a nation aspiring for membership of the Security Council, a place on the high table of the nations, still depending heavily on foreign countries for supply of defence equipments is not good for us."

Economic Times, 29 Feb 2012. http://articles.economictimes.indiatimes.com/2012-02-29/news/31110907_1_piramal-health-care-drug-discovery-pharma-solutions

25 "Piramal Systems, US defence tech firm in talks for joint venture" by Amrita Nair-Ghaswalla, *The Hindu Business Line*, 7 June 2013. http://www.thehindubusinessline.com/companies/piramal-systems-us-defence-tech-firm-in-talks-for-joint-venture/article4791931.ece

26 "Saab inks pact with Piramal Group for land electronic defence system" by Amrita Nair-Ghaswalla, *The Hindu Business Line*, 11 June 2013.
http://m.thehindubusinessline.com/companies/saab-inks-pact-with-piramal-groupfor-land-electronic-defence-system/article4804343.ece/?secid=11680

A trawl through the growing literature on defence will yield this: first, the public sector has failed miserably to deliver, which justifies abandoning the ordnance factories and PSUs and DRDO; second, the private defence industry ought to be given tax benefits and other concessions, preferably a SEZ or two to encourage them to enter this field; only the private sector can attract the talent required for defence innovation and R & D goes the argument, thus naturally requiring a greater cushioning by the government. But since the local industry is not yet ready for taking on these onerous tasks laid out by these well meaning defence analysts, foreign intervention is essential. But since foreign companies will likely not be interested in joint ventures where they have little control owing to the 26 per cent cap on FDI, this 'bottleneck' must be removed.

How ingeniously a case for indigenization is turned into a clarion call for wholesale privatization of the defence sector. Experience and evidence suggest that far from investing in R&D, private sector has been rather shy on this front, with almost the entire R&D in this country being sponsored by the State sector and public institutions. If the influence of the big corporates on India's economic policies, indeed their ability to even install pliant ministers, is any marker, imagine their power to direct the foreign policy, once they become in charge of research, design and manufacturing of weapons and arms. One commentator even argued for greater private role by bringing forth evidence that defence PSU managers "have actually been going out of their way to serve the interests of the foreign 'partner,' rather than the PSU they head".[27]

---

27 "India's Defence needs FDI" by Manoj Joshi, *The Hindu*, 14 May 2013.

Section III

The defence and security industry has been mainstreamed and domesticated by the TV channels by incorporating them under their car and bike shows, where gushing auto reporters, drooling at the size of tyres of Polaris off roaders, speak dreamily about TATA's mine protected vehicles (MPV) advertised to withstand powerful landmines and heavy gun fire in Maoist areas. At least a part of the bloated defence budget would be spent within the country against movements and 'insurgencies'. Tata had already delivered 32 MPVs to Maharashtra State Police and five to Jharkhand Police by 2012.[28]

But the big toys are only part of the story. 'Homeland' security is no small business. If the aforementioned Homeland Security Fair is a purely private affair, INDESEC, one of the earliest in the field, boasts of its association with Ministry of Home Affairs, the principal shopper for these trinkets and tools. The wily pundits at ASSOCHAM smelling an opportunity set up "India's only integrated homeland security and defence systems event" in 2008. This was watershed year for the nascent homeland security market, punctuated as it was by serial blasts across many cities, including Delhi, but the year-end tragedy and madness – memorialized as "26/11"– proved to be truly epoch changing for the industry. The image of flames bellowing out of the Taj Mahal hotel quickly seared itself into what is called the 'national conscience' – a polite euphemism for big media, corporate houses and the right wing inclined political section. It rivaled and replaced the Parliament attack of some years ago as the definitive 9/11 moment of the country.

---

28 http://motorbash.com/tata-delivers-5-mine-protected-vehicles-to-jharkhand-police-force/

From the debris of the Taj emerged several interlocked narratives. The principal of these was outrage. Outrage at violence reaching the Taj Mahal hotel – resurrected as the undisputable icon of India, and even more exaggeratedly as the central civic institution. [29]

> Let's start something guys. A non-cooperation movement to show that we are not taking this lying down. Let it be started by corporates, a nameless, leaderless movement. Lets show the leaders and politicians that we want our safety...

This text message drew hundreds of middle class and well-heeled Mumbaikars to the Gateway of India, leading advertising guru Prahlad Kakkar to gush, "we have never seen such a show of solidarity for a single cause at the gateway of India."[30]

City as the site of violence was hardly new. But with posh seven star hotels turning into battlefields, its heat seemed to have singed those who had remained inured and protected from violence hitherto. India Inc. reacted by quickly and unselfconsciously demanding protection for *itself* – as tax payers, creators of wealth and as citizens. Indeed, there was hardly a distinction between these categories. There was simultaneously a denunciation of the political class, always an inexact category, and the processes of democracy. Industrialists and captains seethed against the politicians first for enjoying "z plus security", and second, for allowing "vote bank politics" to compromise security concerns.

The vantage point from which Simi Garewal, actor and celebrity chat show host, spoke on a TV show was both metaphorical and literal:

---

29 "Invasion of Mumbai", Arvind Adiga, BBC. http://news.bbc.co.uk/2/hi/south_asia/7755149.stm

30 http://www.rediff.com/news/2008/dec/03mumterror-thousands-gather-at-gateway-of-india.htm

> Go to the Four Seasons and look down from the top floor at the slums around you. Do you know what flags you will see? Not the Congress's, not the BJP's, not the Shiv Sena's. Pakistan! Pakistani flags fly high! ... You know what I think? We should carpet-bomb Pakistan. That's the only way we can give a clear message.

Garewal may have apologized later for mistaking Islamic flags for Pakistani, but her belligerent outburst on television encapsulated many of the concerns of "corporate survivors" – a label devised by the business news channel NDTV Profit, not for those who had *survived* the horrible gun fire inside the hotels – the loss of lives at VT station was hardly even discussed – but those who were now left dealing with a battered image of India, especially Mumbai, as a financial and investment destination. It was time, decided NDTV Profit, for these corporate survivors to turn into "corporate activists". Launching a series called Ideas for Change, its Managing Editor espoused:

> Through this campaign we wanted CEOs to use their experience in drafting a blueprint which will help us all to contain this terror. We required ideas from the corporates who till this time have helped in building the shares of their stakeholders and expanding the Indian industry; to provide solutions to issues that would help in safeguarding our country from terrorism.[31]

Egged on by an anchor reminding them of the monies they created for the government, one after another, these corporate survivors/activists vented their indignation against the political establishment, demanded greater public-private partnership in governance (because governments and bureaucracies are corrupt whereas corporates perform better at delivering); called for internal se-

31 "Campaigning against Terror" by Anushree Bhattacharya, Indiantelevision.com, 26 December 2008. http://www.indiantelevision.com/special/y2k8/terror_spl.php

curity to be divorced from Home Ministry, which in thrall to vote bank politics (an established code language for imagined pandering to Muslims) was refusing to take action against terrorists; and finally, a greater investment in security.

Arun Nanda, then executive director of Mahindra and Mahindra, commended more recently for his "grace" and "classic elegance",[32] demanded on the business channel, "accountability not only from people we elect but from people whose salary we pay from our hard-earned money". His big 'idea for change' to achieve this accountability was to break from "Friedman's philosophy of business only as business" and "to start up a body or a union of employees or business people together" and "demand what US did after 9/11, like Homeland Security – an independent body who is not politicized, who is responsible for our children's lives" [sic]. Ajay Piramal – whose Piramal Group was to move into defence and security business a few years later, but then his website describes him as someone "known for identifying opportunities ahead of the curve" – echoed the imperative to follow the example of US which had not experienced any terror attack since 9/11. Vikram Singh Mehta, Chairman of Shell India, and who lived next door to the exclusive Oberoi hotel, could do no better than lift from George Bush: "we should not allow people who are opposed to our way of life."

The litanies of political incompetence and corruption were matched by panicked cries of insecurity. Mohandas Pai of Infosys declared loss of faith in the political leadership which had ensured "z plus security" for itself while leaving the industry to the perils of terror attacks. "What

---

32 "Arun Nanda: The Conscious Capitalist" by Aparna Piramal Raje, 23 June 2013, *Live Mint*. http://www.livemint.com/Leisure/ZrypVAPaHyUeCTdgIuv9aO/Arun-Nanda--The-conscious-capitalist.html

about us? [If] the government is unable to protect us, then amend the law. Let us bear arms, we will protect ourselves to whatever extent we can." Anxious that metal detectors, frisking and CCTV security were too flimsy a foil against automatic weapons and grenades, Kiran Mazumdar Shaw demanded "much stronger help from the government... We'll need military intervention. Maybe we could start some military patrolling at least." Both Pai and Shaw were speaking at a meeting convened by the Karnataka government to reassure an alarmed Industry following the Mumbai attack.[33] And certainly many of these top business houses chose Central Industrial Security Force to guard their premises. Others like DLF in Gurgaon set up their own security company to guard its malls and office complexes – not very different from feudal private armies meant to guard their fiefdom.

But these were not merely the hysterical eruptions of an industry feeling besieged by the possibilities of terror attacks. The public-private partnership in internal security was already well underway by this time. The private security business was proliferating: guarding universities, schools, gated communities, housing societies, malls and business centres. By this time, the Delhi-based Security and Intelligence Services (SIS) had acquired Australia's largest security firm, Chubb Security, which was up for sale, sealing the deal at around $300 million thus becoming the first Indian multinational in the security services industry.[34] The global giant Securitas AB had entered the Indian market in 2007 by acquiring a 49 per cent stake

33 "Give us Guns, India Inc Demands from Govt", CNN IBN, 1 December 2008. ://ibnlive.in.com/news/give-us-guns-india-inc-demands-from-govt/79448-7.html/

34 http://articles.economictimes.indiatimes.com/2013-12-23/news/45510265_1_training-academy-private-security-guards-severance-package

in India's Walsons;[35] companies like Globe, Tops and G4S were huge. However, the bulk of the private security market remained dominated by local and smaller companies. The Private Security Agencies (Regulation) Act (PSARA) was promulgated in 2005 in order to impose some order on this unregulated and fragmented market. In 2006, the Private Security Agencies Central Model Rules were framed for state governments to implement. These rules emphasized training for guards, supervisors and licensees.

The syllabus prescribed by the governments was meant to be wide, straddling physical fitness training, the correct wearing of uniform, fire fighting, crowd control, first aid, identification of improvised explosive devices, firearms, as well as rudimentary knowledge of law (including IPC and how to file an FIR).[36] But all this would require training facilities, equipment, professional trainers – meaning, training would cost money.

Security Post, the newsletter of Central Association of Private Security Industry (CAPSI), carried an editorial on the 'collective action' that was transforming the face of private security industry.

> Nobody among us ever thought that one day many State Governments will join hand with CAPSI to recruit and train security guards for their placement with guarding compa-

---

35 "Mapping the Political Economy of India's Private Security Industry" by Vijay K. Nagaraj, *Economic and Political Weekly*, Vol. XLVII, No 3318, August 2012.

36 See for example, Andhra Pradesh Private Security Agency (Regulation) Rules, 2008, published in the extraordinary issue of the Andhra Pradesh Gazette, dated 22-01-2009. In reply to a question raised in Lok Sabha, the Minister for State for Home Affairs stated in the House that "so far, 31 States/UTs have framed and notified rules based on the provisions of the aforesaid Act and Central Model Rules.
Unstarred Question No. 3666, Answered on 19 March 2013.

> nies, those were always felt starved of educated and trained manpower. The Government of Punjab has started a new academy to train security guards and two batches have already passed out. The DGP of the State Police took the salute of the passing out parade. The State has already agreed to commence diploma and certificate courses for supervisory cadres and for the Security Management. The Government of Rajasthan has signed a MOU with CAPSI to establish Rural Institute of Security Education (RISE) in each district of the State. *Imagine getting well trained manpower from such institutes without spending money*.[37]

The editorial prophesied that this "will provide stability and growth to your business." More state governments were being approached so that members of CAPSI across the country could reap these benefits. But even more happily, skill development and training programmes were being supported by the central government schemes of national rural employment.[38] Elsewhere, the chairman of CAPSI informed that it was "setting up 2,000 security training centres to be funded by state governments."[39]

Very often, the private security industry would market itself as one of the largest employers of rural poor, thus portraying itself as worthy of government benefits and subsidies. At the CAPSI conference, held some

37 *Security Post*, Newsletter of CAPSI and APDI, Vol. 4, May 2008. Emphasis added.

38 In 2011, the TOPSGRUP International Security Academy (TISA) was awarded the contract under the special Swarnajayanti Gram Swarozgar Yojana of Ministry of Rural development to train 30,000 below the poverty line rural youth. In December 2013, the second phase of the star scheme of the Government of India under which the private sector was asked to train 150,000 rural poor as security guards would be launched at CAPSI's annual conference.

39 "Security Guards become the Frontline in India" by Heather Timmons, 2 March 2009, *New York Times*. http://www.nytimes.com/2009/03/03/business/worldbusiness/03security.html

months after the above-cited newsletter was published – and a mere month and a half before Mumbai happened – the private security industry plugged its preeminence as a job generator. Speaking at the same conference, the then Home Minister Shivraj Patil, admitted that he was "flabbergasted" to learn that "55 lakh men are working as guards and officers in private agency". [sic][40] In absence of a high police to people ratio, the ubiquitous private guard began to be touted as an alternative to the police. It was another matter that this workforce was blighted by low wages, long and strenuous working hours, little social or job security.[41] One security company advertised its services thus: "We Proudly declare that we have never faced any labour unrest within our force. Our employees are strictly prohibited to join any union. They are also not allowed to mix with other undesirable elements."[42]

With 26/11, these comparatively sober arguments of the private security industry gave way to a more frenzied rhetoric. The chorus for private security to augment counterterrorism operations grew louder. Unsurprisingly, the attacks accelerated the already fast growing industry. From 22-25 percent growth rate, it was expected to jump to now 30-35, or even 40 per cent.[43]

---

40 http://www.capsi.in/images/speeches.pdf

41 *Labour, Employment and Social Security Issues of Security Guards Engaged by Private Security Agencies: A Case Study of Okhla and Noida* by Sanjay Upadhyaya, NLI Research Studies Series, 093/2011, VV Giri National Labour Institute, 2011.

42 Vigilant Corporate Services, formerly Continental Security Group, Gurgaon. http://www.indiamart.com/vc-services-pvtltd/

43 "Security Firms Reap Dividends on Social Unrest, Terrorism" by Pramudgha Mamgain and Rajat Guha, *ET Bureau*, 6 November 2008. http://articles.indiatimes.com/2008-11-06/news/28474046_1_private-security-security-concerns-security-personnel; and also see "Terror Flipside: 40 % Growth in pvt security job market" by Raghvendra Rao, *Indian Express*, 25

Barely a fortnight after the attacks, Federation of Indian Chamber of Commerce and Industry (FICCI) organized a national conference on national security and terrorism in Delhi, attended by the who's who of the security establishment: B. Raman, Ajit Doval, Brijesh Mishra among others. From the conference emerged "a series of action points" which then were elaborated in a Task Force Report.[44] Quoting the 9/11 Commission, which had outlined the "cost of doing business in a post 9/11 world", the report exhorted the Indian business community to prepare for the threat to "the luxury hotels that house foreign investors, the cafes that play host to all nationalities and the markets that sell the new India's success story". To the government it warned that national counterterrorism mechanism were essential to retain "foreign investment".[45]

It echoed the views of the industry heads – but naturally – that private establishments urgently required armed protection. However, the laws governing private security establishments stood in the way of managements to equip their "private security with modern weapons freely accessible to terrorist". Private security firms wanted the removal of this legal hurdle to raise private militias – of course only for those companies whose turnover crossed 100 crores – but also wanted tax relief for "enhancing security".

It was also coincidental that from mid 2000s, the industrial belts, especially in Haryana and Rajasthan had been witnessing a restive labour force, increasingly de-

---

March 2009. Access at: http://expressindia.indianexpress.com/story.php?storyId=438582

44 *Task Force Report on National Secrity and Terrorism*, Vol. 1, Federation of Indian Chamber of Commerce and Industry, New Delhi, 2009.

45 Ibid., p. 88.

manding its right to unionize. This workforce had to be disciplined too.

Section IV

India Inc. had pronounced the onset of the "era of Mumbai terror".[46] New waves of "Jihadi fighters" were expected to spring from every turn and corner.

But every tragedy has the potential for profiteering. The Mumbai carnage triggered an unprecedented demand for security solutions. The coastlines had to be secured; the army and police modernized, cities monitored and populations mapped and accounted for. Airports, shopping malls, schools, streets – the swathes which had to be secured were limitless.

The FICCI conference was only the first. Consultancy firms and business and trade bodies held conferences and symposia, conducted surveys and assessments, produced voluminous reports, petitioned, advised, cajoled and prescribed policy to the government. Internal security, long the preserve of the Ministry of Home Affairs, mutated into Homeland Security. It wasn't simply the arrival of a new terminology and lexicon; it also marked the unveiling of a new techno-security state, advocated feverishly by an elastic group of corporates, ex-army generals, technocrats, arms traders, think tanks, security experts, commentators – and it was difficult mostly to tell one from another.

First, there was an assessment to make. Of the spoils that were to be had from this unprecedented expansion of market that 26/11 had spurred. There was suddenly a glut of reports and papers accounting the monies to be made from this unexpected opportunity.

46 *FICCI Task Force Report*, p. 50.

You can almost sense them licking their lips and rubbing their hands as they tally up the "scope" of coverage in critical infrastructure protection ("very large and diversified"...to the tune of USD 10 bn over the next 4-5 years"), fencing along Indo-Bangladesh border ("Rs 800 crores opportunity"); salivated at the outlays for border security initiatives (Rs 969.69 crores) for improving coastal security, for counterinsurgency and anti-terrorists schools, as well as for development of "infrastructure to address left wing extremism". And then there were projections about the emergent "Intelligence Cyber technology, security networks and identification" market arising from Natgrid, National Population Register, Unique Identification Card, centralised monitoring systems, lawful interception, biometric use in census – all new initiatives undertaken post 2008 – to keep the HS crowd excited.[47]

And if this burgeoning market wasn't large enough, it had to be forged through the rhetoric of war and security. Introducing the FICCI Task Force Report, MP and chairman of the Task Force, Rajeev Chandrashekhar wrote:

> 26/11 was an unprecedented attack on our nation. It reinforced the often forgotten fact, that we have a war being waged against us. The difference was 26/11 was an attack on the economic centers and establishment of our country. We have all come to realize that if left unchecked, this growing threat has the potential to derail our economic and social progress. On the one hand, some of our neighbours have combined conventional military wisdom and statecraft to support terrorist organisations that are determined to bleed India. On the other, naxalism and Maoist violence is spreading. *It is a crisis unparalleled in the history of young India*.[48]

---

47 *Homeland Security Assessment – India, Expansion and Growth*; Thought Leadership series, Assocham India and Aviotech, June 2011.

48 *FICCI Task Force Report*, p. 5, Emphasis added.

An unparalleled crisis, naturally, demands unparalleled measures. In calling for a "national counterterrorism architecture" which would include a new legislative framework, creation of new agencies and mechanisms, the deployment of emergent technologies, and a hawkish foreign policy, this report comprehensively lays down the ideological bedrock of HS in India. The blueprint for this architectural design is borrowed wholesale from the US. Therefore, setting up of National Intelligence Agency through an act of Parliament and amendments in the Unlawful Activity Prevention Act, "which would, inter alia, allow for the detention of terror suspects up to 180 days" in the immediate aftermath of the tragedy, are lauded as important steps, but viewed as ultimately inadequate to "substantially enhance our capability to counter terror". Lamenting the fissiparous tendencies of the country's multiple intelligence and law enforcement agencies, it conceives of – drawing from US experience of course – the National Counter Terror Agency (NCTA), only replacing 'centre' with 'agency' here, as a mark of tropicalization, perhaps. The demand for "an overarching institution to address internal security" has been raised repeatedly by reports of think tanks, even as recently as the summer of 2013, much after the idea of NCTC had been mauled as infringing upon the federal rights of the states.[49]

The NCTC's function is conceived much like that of a cosmic blender, which combines, collates, refines and spews out information and intelligence on the one hand, and on the other the only agency empowered to act and coordinate all terror investigations. Not only would

49 *Building a Lasting Partnership via Transportation Sector Security*, A Report of the Homeland Security and Counterterrorism Program, Centre for International and Strategic Studies, Washington, June 2013. http://csis.org/files/publication/130618_Nelson_US-IndiaHomeland_WEB.pdf

its Director General coordinate with National Intelligence Agency and head the National Intelligence Grid, but would also "be empowered to maintain liaisons with friendly security and counter terrorist agencies". The Report asks for this all-powerful NCTA's imbrication with the Intelligence Bureau, a body itself on very shaky legal ground.

Above all, FICCI Task Force's principle recipe for counterterrorism is invasive technology. Mesmerized again by the US' leveraging of IT as a "key weapon in the war against terror", the Report laments the wasting of vast amounts of personal information which lies unutilized in the isolated silos of banks, credit card companies, telephone companies, and in the trail of transactions made by every individual, which could have been harnessed by a "more integrated public surveillance system" to allow for the "seamless flow of information from one silo to another".[50] That the US Department of Homeland Security (DHS) spent 3.75 Bn USD in 2004 and more than 11 Bn USD in 2005 in creating these common information and attendant data mining systems could be seen as an added incentive for the corporate sector to push for these excessive technological solutions. While these agencies may still have been in the realm of proposals and wishful thinking, the Report made a case for something that was more immediate: absorbing the data being produced by Nandan Nilekeni's UIDAI "as part of National grid to assist in counterterrorism".[51] The ASSOCHAM-Aviotech report of 2011 gleefully noted that the UID project would create "business opportunities worth INR 6,500 (USD 1.44) in the first phase of implementation. A budget of INR 1470 Cr has been allocated during annual plan 2011-

50 *FICCI Task Force Report*, p. 68.

51 Ibid., p. 70.

12."[52] The Government may have been advertising UID as part of its welfarist package – as the ultimate corruption-free passport to services and schemes[53] – it's uses as a money- spinner for the industry and surveillance tool for the security agencies were always on the surface.

If the folks at FICCI were at all anxious that agencies modeled after the US National Information Exchange Model (NIEM), which facilitates data sharing beyond law enforcement, and Homeland Security Information Network (HSIN), which makes data available from any computer terminal, would infringe upon the privacy and rights of citizens, the Chairman of the Task Force had already elaborated in his Notes from the Conference held in 2008 that the war on terror could not be won "without sacrifices". "National interest" is paramount and should prevail over any "other interests" *even if they are constitutionally and democratically valid*."[54] Indeed, the Report emphasizes that the private sector "must support laws which may well entail invasion of privacy in order to make surveillance and monitoring effective".[55]

It's a frightening coalescing of corporate greed and an authoritarian vision of the state.

(We may add here that Chandrashekhar, chairman of the FICCI Task Force – and also a member of the Standing Committee on Finance headed by Yashwant Sinha which opposed the UID tooth and nail on grounds of national security – began in 2014 to debunk the UID

---

52 *Homeland Security Assessment – India, Expansion and Growth*, ASSOCHAM and Aviotech, Delhi, 2011.

53 For a critique of the supposed welfarism of UID, see *This or That Particular Person*, a film by Subrasri Krishnan, Produced by Public Service Broadcasting Trust, 2012.

54 *FICCI Task Report,* p. 115, emphasis added.

55 Ibid., p. 101.

scheme as unnecessary and costly hype besides being a threat to individual privacy and national security, as the UID did not differentiate between citizens and illegal immigrants.[56] His views came to be favoured by the policy makers at the right wing Niti Central,[57] which advocated the replacement of the UID with the National Identity Number linked to the National Population Register. The UID in this view is a weak security tool which needs to be replaced with a more efficient one. In its maiden budget the Modi government allocated Rs 2039 crores in the first fiscal, despite BJP's blusterous opposition to UID during the UPA years.[58])

Though FICCI calls upon the civil society to intervene in this process, even asking them to engage in a dialogue with armed groups, and argues for the indispensability of human rights framework – it becomes increasingly clear that FICCI imagines the civil society as a handmaiden in its Project Counterterrorism: its principal role being to conduct statistical and empirical research into the causes of terrorism (without of course "according any legiti-

---

56 "The UID: Gamechanger or Hype" by Rajeev Chandrashekhar; *Open Magazine*, 6 February 2014. http://www.openthemagazine.com/political_hotline/power-blog/the-uid-gamechanger-or-hype

57 See "Nilekani's Aadhaar a Danger to our Privacy" by Sandhya Jain, *Niti Central*, 13 March 2014. (http://www.niticentral.com/2014/03/13/nilekanis-aadhaar-a-danger-to-our-privacy-199690.html). Also, "Narendra Modi must Reboot Aadhaar Scheme" by Avinash Sharma, *Niti Central,* 5 July 2014. http://www.niticentral.com/2014/06/17/narendra-modi-must-reboot-aadhaar-scheme-231800.html. The new government dissolved the Cabinet Committee on Unique Identification Authority of India soon after taking over. "Out with the Old: Narendra Modi disbands four Cabinet Committees", *DNA*, 11 June 2014. http://www.dnaindia.com/india/report-out-with-the-old-narendra-modi-disbands-four-cabinet-committees-1994741

58 "Modi Govt to give Legal Backing to Aadhaar", *Times of India*, 14 July, 2014.

macy to the perpetrators of violence"); to humanize the war against terror by "maintaining a principled approach to the applicability of human rights standards, i.e., these standards apply to both perpetrators and victims of violence", to liaise with media to "shape the public discourse around terrorism".[59]

But FICCI gets burdened by its own rhetoric of human rights and swiftly condemns the same civil society, which "in reality [seems] to function more as a body to criticize every governmental move, and give greater importance to forces threatening the secular fabric of the country or other negative forces. ... A code of ethics for their functioning needs to be evolved... and any of these organisations breaching this code should be brought to book mercilessly..."[60]

Criticism of the government is thus anathema, and wasting time on battling communalism is to be avoided. To the civil society, the Report recommends that it promote "positive vibes between the police and the people instead of making mockery of the police"; and following the Israeli model, engage itself in motivating the public to cooperate with the inconveniences of security procedures (because "people need to be disciplined in order to avoid bloodshed"); and support moves for provision for every visitor's details by hotels, guest houses, and even "*personal guests to local police*". Of course it would help if the government were to include security in the academic curriculum, schooling young minds in the need for such a regime; and further, if employment in government sector be made contingent on some years of compulsory service

59 *FICCI Task Force Report*, p. 97.

60 Ibid., p. 99.

in the armed forces.[61] (Though the private sector will do fine without this compulsory service.)

In its vision then, the role for each agency and institution is clearly defined: the private sector to develop the technologies of discipline and surveillance; the government to create the pseudo-legal apparatus of this techno-security state; and the civil society to create a pliant and disciplined citizenry.

The sense of grandeur and delusion is not missing altogether. Advocacy of closer ties with US, both strategic and economic, is accompanied by cries for a foreign policy that mimics the US': covert operations, surgical strikes and all-out assault against Pakistan are highly recommended.[62] Ignore the lack of irony in suffixing India's "commitment to global peace and prosperity" with it's "expeditionary military capabilities," the FICCI Report makes it clear that it desires for India's absorption into 'International community' (one of the names by which NATO goes) to fight terrorism "outside its geographical boundaries".[63] This must be read in the light of so-called International community's attempts to draw India into its increasingly loss-making Afghanistan war.

The Task Force Report serves as the ideological template of the numerous Industry reports and surveys that followed. An offering by FICCI and Ernst & Young on "Building Safe and Secure Indian Cities", made this stunning observation: "In India, violence stems from incidents of terrorism in cities." But then its definition of a safe city is also rather original: "In essence", it says, "in a safe and liveable city, the market forces of demand and

61 Ibid., p. 55.

62 pp. 48-9.

63 p. 60.

supply are able to operate efficiently to generate an efficient economy model."[64]

In addition to terrorism, which drives away investors, the market forces are also obstructed by crime. Outlining the key risk factors – inadequate living conditions, poverty, poor parenting and alcohol abuse, poor school performance, optimal functioning of schools, lack of employment opportunities – *Building Safe and Secure Cities* envisages a city at threat from the underclass – indeed it criminalizes poverty itself. The solutions it offers are consistent with such a view of urban violence. It argues, ingeniously it thinks, for CPTED (Crime Prevention through Environmental Design). This is basically a fancy term for creating exclusive enclaves to keep out populations marked as potentially offensive and suspect through denial of access, manned security and such like. The second solution is totalizing surveillance technology including centralized data system, GIS-based analysis and reporting, and the ubiquitous CCTV camera.

ASSOCHAM-Aviotech's *Homeland Security Assessment* reported how city surveillance projects in Delhi and Mumbai would present a business opportunity outstripping USD 100 mn.

There was an enthusiastic embracing of surveillance cameras across the country with government directing private institutions to deploy CCTVs. Malls, banks, cyber cafes, hotels and guest-houses, colleges and universities installed these cameras with or without these directives.[65]

---

64 *Building Safe and Secure Indian Cities -- A Perspective, Homeland Security 2011*, Ernst & Young Pvt. Ltd. and FICCI, Kolkata, 2011.

65 See Privacy International's survey of India's surveillance policies at: https://www.privacyinternational.org/reports/india/iii-surveillance-policies#footnote29_y60w93z. Terrorist threats as well as

Building Safe and Secure Cities,[66] Wipro's whitepaper underlines the need for "integrated solutions for a safe city" and lauds the London model (which incidentally has more CCTV cameras per person than anywhere else, and according to a study, a busy Londoner was likely to be captured on a CCTV almost 300 times a day,[67] so pervasive was the network) and welcomes the Safe Surat project. But to call it a whitepaper is a misnomer for it is little more than a brochure advertising Wipro's goods and services including video surveillance, facial recognition systems, and applications to analyze, sort and store this data. China's multi-billion 500,000 cameras security system in the megacity of Chongquing is also hailed as a great stride forward in securing cities through technology.[68]

In India, the closest one comes to the London model, yet, is the Safe City Surat project.[69] In its first phase, inaugurated by "the great leader" Narendra Modi in January 2013, 104 CCTVs have been installed at 23 points across the city. A dedicated optical fibre channel connects the cameras to each, feeding a massive 280 square foot "video wall" at the Command, Control and Communications center (C3). The data is stored in IBM computers (data storage, management and disposal is by itself another lucrative and emerging market) while the video cameras come from Verint Systems, an Israeli company known to

---

disquiet over localized crimes have spurred CCTV proliferation in both private institutions and public spaces and open streets.

66 *Building Safe and Secure Cities* by Chockalingam Chidambaram, Wipro Infotech, Bangalore, 2013.

67 *The Maximum Suveillance Society: The Rise of CCTV* by Clive Norris and Gary Armstrong, Berg, New York, 1999.

68 *Building Safe and Secure Cities – A Perspective, Homeland Security 2011*, FICCI and Ernst and Young, Kolkata, 2011, p. 23.

69 http://www.safecitysurat.com/

be close to its intelligence agency. As an aside, one may note that Verint has also been accused of illegally wire-trapping Verizon phones in the US for NSA.[70]

Safe City Surat imitates the British surveillance system in more ways than one. It is born out of a partnership between local business elites, police and authorities, just as in 1993, following the famous Bulger case, the British Home Secretary announced the allocation of £2 million of central government money for open street CCTV, to be won by bidding if cities could demonstrate matched funding from alternative sources.[71] R.K. Asthana, the Police Commissioner in the aftermath of the blasts in Zaveri Bazar, the diamond market of Mumbai, in 2011, authored the scheme; diamond merchants of Surat raised the money; Surat Traffic Education managed funds. And thus was scripted another giddy story celebrating the 'Gujarat model of doing things'. By the conclusion of this "fine example of police-public-private partnership", 5000 surveillance cameras at over 500 locations in the city would be installed.[72]

---

70 "Shady Companies with Ties to Israel Wiretrap the US for NSA" by James Bamford, *Wired Magazine*, http://www.wired.com/threatlevel/2012/04/shady-companies-nsa/all/1

71 Fuzzy CCTV images of a toddler Jamie Bulger being led to his death by two ten-year-olds in a shopping mall were broadcast repeatedly by television channels, unleashing not only a national and collective panic over juvenile crime, but also a demand for CCTV cameras as security apparatus. See "The Growth of CCTV: a global perspective on the international diffusion of video surveillance in publicly accessible space" by Clive Norris, Mike McCahill and David Wood, special double issue of *Surveillance & Society*, 2(2/3): 110-135.

72 http://www.rediff.com/news/slide-show/slide-show-1-citizens-and-police-unite-for-surats-third-eye/20130531.htm; see also http://articles.timesofindia.indiatimes.com/2013-01-19/infrastructure/36431332_1_surat-traffic-education-trust-surveillance-system-innovative-telecom

Described by Modi as Surat's 'third eye', the system would be used to combat Mumbai-type terror attack, as much as traffic offenders and criminals. Asthana paints a picture of the city overtaken by migrants and crime, the laidback Surati lala edged out by cutthroat migrants, creating the "unavoidable necessity of having better surveillance and security".

This agitation about migrants, traffic offenders and terrorists is part of a new managerial penology, in which risks are to be identified (created and hyped in many cases) and eliminated *before* a crime. Numerous risk surveys conducted by consultancy firms attest to the rise of this actuarialism. The FICCI-Pinkerton India Risk Survey 2012 sets out to quantify "potentially destructive risks to the business enterprises of the country" in the backdrop of the "global economic meltdown".[73] The risks enumerated in the Survey range from terrorism, cyber insecurity, fire, political instability, to strikes and workers' violence. Now part of AB Securitas, the world's largest security company, Pinkerton's illustrious history of 'risk management' includes breaking strikes on behalf of the US government in the 19th century that continued till the passage of Anti Pinkerton Act by the US Congress in 1893 to curtail the government's powers of breaking strikes.[74] The Act prohibits the government of the United States or the government of the District of Columbia from employing an individual hired by the Pinkerton Detective Agency, or similar organization.

Terrorism has emerged as a kind of hold-all in which specific threats can be accommodated. A report by Reli-

---

73 *India Risk Survey 2012* by FICCI and Pinkerton Consulting & Investigations India Pvt. Ltd., Delhi, 2012.

74 Pub. L. 89– 554, Sept. 6, 1966, 80 Stat. 416. See http://uscode.house.gov/view.xhtml?req=granuleid:USC-prelim-title5-section3108&num=0&edition=prelim

ance-owned Observer Research Foundation (in partnership with the UK thinktank RUSI) focused on security risks associated with chemical, biological and radiological materials (CBR).[75] The report tries desperately to link CBR with terrorism, simultaneously participating in the terror paranoia and feeding it. It harps on an incident of cyanide poisoning of a woman by suspected Laskar-e Tayyaba militants in Kashmir to hardsell a policy shift from safety to security. The path to this transition is to create an overarching legislative framework on the pattern of – no prizes for guessing – the US. Nuclear Disaster Preparedness Act 2011, Chemical Facility Anti Terrorism Security Authorization Act 2011 etc.[76]

ORF's website no longer lists Lockheed Martin or Raytheon as its partners[77] though a little more search will yield that the relationship has continued. ORF's joint workshop with National Bureau of Asian Research on India's Strategic Environment and Defence Policies was supported by US defence companies Lockheed Martin, Boeing and Northrop Grumann.[78] Among the workshop's other sponsors was the Lynde and Harry Bradley Foundation, an arch right wing foundation that aggressively pushes racist and Islamophobic writers and publications, funds commentators and think tanks who advocate a belligerent US foreign policy, and organizations that attack

---

75 *Chemical, Biological and Radiological Materials: An Analysis of Security Risks and Terrorist Threats to India*, Observer Research Foundation, Delhi, 2012.

76 Ibid., p. 29.

77 "Capitalism: A Ghost Story" by Arundhati Roy, 26 March 2012, *Outlook*.

78 Dates of workshop: April 23-25 2009. In *The US India Defence Relationship: An Update for President Obama's Visit to India, November 2010*, NBR, Washington, 2010. http://www.nbr.org/downloads/pdfs/PSA/PR_US-India_Workshop.pdf

public funding of education and renewable sources of energy.[79]

More recently, the Cyber Security and Cyber Governance Conference organised by ORF and FICCI received the support of Raytheon.[80] In case one is wondering why a big weapons company would be interested in cyber governance in India, it might be worth knowing that Raytheon is said to have developed a new 'RIOT' software (Rapid Information Overlay Technology in plain language) which has the ability to mine data from social networking sites to track individuals, and also to predict their daily routines and practices in the near future. "We know where Nick's been, what he looks like and where he might be headed", cooed a pleased Raytheon employee in a demo CD. The technology has been shown to the US government and industry but not yet sold.[81]

A report on transportation security published by Centre for the Strategic and International Studies (CSIS) mentions Godhra train burning (strictly as the trigger for largescale violence) but is amnesiac about the Samjhauta

---

79 *Buying a Movement: Right-wing Foundations and American Politics*, not dated, access at http://www.pfaw.org/sites/default/files/buyingamovement.pdf; also see *P is for Payoff: Inside the Bradley Foundation's Campaign to Privatize Education in Wisconsin*, One Wisconsin, April 2013 (Access at http://www.onewisconsinnow.org/p-is-for-payoff.pdf) and "Secret funding helped build vast network of climate denial thinktanks" by Suzanne Goldenberg, *The Guardian*, 14 February 2013 at http://www.theguardian.com/environment/2013/feb/14/funding-climate-change-denial-thinktanks-network

80 http://orfonline.org/cms/export/orfonline/img/cyfyn/speeches-mr-sunjoy-joshi.html; Dates of Conference: 14-15 October 2013.

81 "Software that Tracks People on Social Media Created by Defence Firm" by Ryan Gallaghar, *The Guardian*, 10 February 2013. http://www.theguardian.com/world/2013/feb/10/software-tracks-social-media-defence. View the video at http://www.engadget.com/2013/02/11/raytheon-riot-software-online-spying/

Express bombings.[82] It predictably concludes with an appeal and a fervent wish for greater cooperation not only between government agencies, but also among the private sectors of US and India.

But as usual, the back-story can be more fascinating. A child of the Cold war era, CSIS, the report's publisher, is ranked fifth in the global hierarchy of think tanks[83] and assigned the top spot among think tanks that work on security and international affairs.[84] Its self-proclaimed mandate is to find "ways to sustain American prominence and prosperity as a force for good in the world".

The Transport Security Report's brief acknowledgements thank Security Watch India for research assistance and General Dynamics Corporation for the generous financial support. SWI is a consultancy firm cum wannabe think tank, which regularly organizes conferences on themes of homeland security. It is 'mentored' by Maroof Raza, made famous by his ability to outshout the Pakistani generals night after night on the truculent Times Now shows hosted by the ever bellicose and hyper nationalist Arnab Goswami. In 2012, a complaint was filed with the National Broadcasters Association that Maroof Raza's appearance as a defence and security analyst commenting on the Indian Army's Tatra trucks deal was a conflict of

---

82 *Building a Lasting Partnership via Transportation Sector Security*, A Report of the Homeland Security and Counterterrorism Program, Centre for International and Strategic Studies, Washington, June 2013. http://csis.org/files/publication/130618_Nelson_US-IndiaHomeland_WEB.pdf, pp. 6-7.

83 *2012 Global Go to Think Tanks Index Report* by James G. McGann, Think Tanks and Civil Society Program and International Relations Program, University of Pennsylvania, January 2013. http://repository.upenn.edu/cgi/viewcontent.cgi?article=1006&context=think_tanks, Table No. 13, p. 66.

84 Ibid., Table No. 3, p. 45.

interest since his firm M/s Maroof Raza & Associates was an agent for several foreign arms manufacturers and dealers. The NBA finding credence in the complaint, adjudicated that his comments could have been coloured by the interests of his clients and directed that Times Now disclose the business interests of this expert panelist.[85] Last heard, Mr. Raza of M/s Maroof Raza & Associates had begun anchoring a special show on strategic affairs called Latitude. As for the financers of this 'study', General Dynamics, described on its website as the market leader in business aviation, land combat and marine systems, has pretty much all elements covered.

These capillaries of think-tanks – India is now home to the fourth largest number of think tanks, trailing behind only USA, China and UK – defence companies, and industry with cross cutting interests have spun so fine a web that it is sometimes difficult to decipher who is who.

Are fears of a totalitarian society and *Nineteen Eighty Four*-esque State unfounded? Remember that these surveillance practices would be conjoined with ideological assumptions about 'dangerous classes'/'potential offenders', as well as elitist exclusionary spatial strategies. Remember also that it is not simply a big brother panoptic camera eye that watches over us (the data offered up by CCTVs has been often found to be grainy and unreliable); it is enmeshed with many other newly emerging techniques such as the centralized monitoring system which will enable every call from a landline or a mobile phone to be snooped upon, and every text message, email and internet search history to be collected and scrutinized.[86] And finally, the arrival in India of companies like Verint with

85 Summary of NBA order dated 25 October 2012. Copy on record.

86 "Architecture of Surveillance" by SAHRDC, *Economic and Political Weekly*, Vol. XLIX, No. 1, 4 January 2014, pp. 10-12.

dubious pasts and Raytheon with scary technology, compounded by think tanks plumped like leeches on blood money from the defence industry or ideologically conservative funders hawk war and terrorism in their policy papers, briefs and television discussions.

From the furnace of this ideological and corporate interest is being minted the vision of a new state.

Appendices

Stories from Kafkaland

I. Letter of condolence to the victims of the blasts from the victims of State terrorism

II. Irshad Ali's letter to the Prime Minister from high security ward, Tihar Jail

III. Excerpts from the judgement in Andhra Pradesh Civil Liberties Committee versus the Government of Andhra Pradesh, by the High Court of Judicature of Andhra Pradesh at Hyderabad (Special Original Jurisdiction)

IV. Extract from the judgement in *State vs Saqib Rehman alias Masood and others* pronounced in the Court of Additional Sessions Judge Virender Bhat

Appendix I

Thirteen men, alleged to be members of SIMI, were charged with planning and executing the bomb blasts that ripped through the local trains in Mumbai on 11 July 2006. Their lawyer, the late Advocate Shahid Azmi, circulated this letter from his clients in 2008. It was titled, "Letter of condolence to the victims of the blasts from the victims of State terrorism".

July 11, 2006 remains an unforgotten day of horrific events in people's mind. Seven blasts in first class coaches of Mumbai's local trains moved the entire nation and global community. 187 innocents died and about 817 people were injured. Condemnation poured from all quarters. It was only due to utter lethargy of the inept administration and security agencies that a cowardice act of terror ripped apart many lives and left a deep wound in the hearts of many. The advent of 11th of July once again opens the wounds of the victims of terror. Had the administration and the security agencies done their work properly rising above all petty political issues, such a disaster would have been certainly prevented. This would have led to an atmosphere of peace and fearlessness. Alas, we can only pray for peace and tranquillity.

You have been the victims of the conspiracies of the terrorists and we are the victims of a different kind of terror – STATE TERRORISM. We are victimised for no fault of ours and have been forced to spend the best days of our youth behind bars.

Your relatives are the victims of the blast, and we are the victims of the inquiry of the blasts. The souls of 187 people might be longing to see that their murderers are brought to book and punished. 817 people had been injured still the ATS has been turning a blind eye towards the actual culprits, have arrested innocent youth and put them behind bars with a sole aim of winning accolades of solving the case.

We, thirteen – innocent accused, are with you in this time of the grief and remembrance. We request you not to consider us as murderers, but victims who are suffering for a deed with which they have no connection at all. We are not a part of any conspiracy, nor are we associated in any way with Lashkar-e Tayyaba. We have not even seen any al-Qaeda manual, we are not bomb makers nor are we the planters. To be true we have not committed any crime nor have we given any confession.

ATS has just played this game with the sole aim of silencing the public and the so called leaders and to diffuse the atmosphere of fear that had been created. Unfortunately, the perpetrators of the terror are still roaming free. The truth is that the ATS remained clueless (intentionally or unintentionally) and we were made the scapegoats so that they heave a sigh of relief. No doubt you are suffering for the loss of your near and dear ones, but we are suffering each moment for the last two years.

We here behind bars and our family members outside are suffering daily running from pillar to post with a sole aim to prove our innocence. Innocent young men, professionals like Doctor, Teacher, Engineer, Software engineer, Call Centre Executive, etc are living along with criminals in jail. Though innocent, we have to listen to insults such as traitor, killer, terrorists by people who are known criminals and serving their jail terms for heinous crimes like rape, murder and dacoity. We face anger and hatred from other inmates and jail authorities. There are very few facilities given in jail and we are subjected to more harassment on the directions of ATS. The jail authorities too are prejudiced everywhere.

For the last one year, the accused have faced torture at the hands of the ATS and now they are undergoing mental agony in jail. They have been divided into small groups and lodged in

Arthur Road jail in different barracks; home to many hardcore criminals. ATS was pressurising each one to turn approver in the case, but the accused have remained steadfast and strongly believe that the truth will prevail. They are hopeful of understanding and support from the people who stand up for truth and justice.

Appendix II

On 9 February 2006, the Delhi Police Special Cell 'arrested' Maurif Qamar and Md. Irshad Ali, accusing them of being the operatives of a terrorist organization, Al Badr. Qamar and Ali moved the High Court seeking a CBI probe, which was granted. The CBI investigations showed that both were actually police informers who were assigned the task of infiltrating terrorist organizations in Jammu and Kashmir. Irshad Ali wrote this letter to the Prime Minister while lodged in the high security cell of the Tihar jail. Iftikhar Gilani has translated it into English from the original Urdu.

The Prime Minister of India
South Block

Dear Sir,

I am writing this letter from the confinement of Tihar Jail with the aim to save innocent youth from getting trapped into the net woven by unscrupulous men in the security agencies to earn rewards and promotions in the name of fighting terrorism. I hope it will help people and your readers and enable them to largely save themselves. Let me introduce myself. My name is Irshad Ali S/o Mohamamd Yunus incarcerated in Ward No. 5 (High Risk Ward) Cell No. 13 in Jail No. 8 of Delhi's Tihar Jail.

Many of you may have recently read my story in The Times of India dated September 13, 2007 citing a CBI report confirming that IB and Special Cell of Delhi Police had framed us. But, I suspect if the CBI report goes further and nails the actual culprits.

I was working as an Informer for the Special Cell of Delhi Police, which works closely with the IB to nab terrorists. Having worked closely with them, I feel duty bound to appraise the nation of the working of these agencies and how they manufacture terrorists. They have made the war on terrorism a total farce. Have you ever noticed how quick our agencies are in nabbing the culprits even before they strike? But, how interesting it is that still they have not yet been able to lay their hands on any terrorist involved in Mumbai and Delhi blasts? Why? I have answers.

In order to keep their ranks and earn rewards, Special Cell creates terrorists. I will tell you how these agencies work. They have employed a number of youth, on a very paltry remuneration. They are not regular employees, but just vagabonds, who are given mobile phones and protection. They are asked to fan out and hire accommodation somewhere in the city. They mingle with unemployed youth and befriend people around. After identifying vulnerable targets, they form a group, arrange weapons and incite these youth to go for a robbery. Special Cell secretively also provides them a stolen vehicle, which is procured from known car thieves.

These youth who vest all their trust in the Special Cell agent finally one day decide to go for an operation. Upon reaching the target, they are trapped in the net, like a fish. At the targeted place, Police is already there to receive them and they are all nabbed without resistance. Interestingly, the agent, who is also a mastermind, never gets in police trap and he successfully vanishes. Medals and bravery awards follow.

An interesting aspect of this whole episode remains that these youth never realize the truth behind their arrest. They curse their luck and resign to their fate spending years in imprisonment.

Now, let me shed some light on the working of the Intelligence Bureau (IB). This is the most useless agency which does nothing, but to feed the government and media with concocted stories. That earns them crores of rupees from the government besides special powers. And they are least accountable because every thing is done in a secretive manner. You may have heard often stories like; a dozen terrorists have landed in Delhi; half-a-dozen terrorists are roaming in Mumbai; ISI is taking roots in UP etc.

Now to back their claims, a Maulvi type agent sporting a long beard and well versed with Islamic tenets is launched in some Muslim locality. Most often, the Maulvi either takes a rented accommodation near a mosque or in some cases makes mosque itself an abode. The pious nature of the Maulvi, his praying five times a day and some heart-rending story easily earns him sympathy and attention. He starts befriending particularly educated Muslim youth. Slowly he identifies targets, harangues them with anti-India and anti-government lectures, laments over condition of Muslims and emphasizes the need for waging jihad.

One day, he confides to the group, that he was actually a Commander of Lashkar-e Tayyaba (LeT) or some other organization. These youth, who are already brainwashed and enticed, now a in fit of emotions believe in the agent. Small weapons are distributed amongst them with a partial training of their working. Meanwhile, ammunition and vehicles and other things arrive. The agent is in touch with the sleuths in the IB and reports to them with minute to minute happenings.

Finally, when the stage is set, the Commander calls for an operation. Even a recce is done. Meanwhile, the IB informs the Special Cell, who put a trap at the targeted place. These youth fall in their lap like ripe fruits without any resistance along with arms and ammunition. They never know how they got into the police net. When police raids to nab their Commander, he is already back with the IB to explore newer pastures. He is never found. A terse news follows that so many terrorists were arrested and one managed to give police a slip.

These trapped youth curse themselves and feel guilty for rest of their life. Special Cell officers tell them that their crimes demand that they be killed in fake encounter, but having mercy on them, "we will send you to jail, where you will get out within six, seven years." These people also remain indebted to police, without knowing the background.

There are also cases where police plants incriminatory things like explosives, drugs on the detainees. The question remains where they get such things. It is quite easy. For example, if someone is caught with a fake currency Rs. 50 lakh. Since the punishment for Rs. 50 lakh or five lakh is same, it does not matter for the Police whether to charge the accused for a lower or a higher sum. They will charge the accused for just Rs. 5 lakh, who for lack of knowledge of law also remains indebted to them. Rest Rs. 45 lakh fake currency is deposited in the safe confines and later planted on victims. Same is the case with smack, heroin, explosives and everything.

Both the Special Cell and the IB have procured huge farm houses in the vicinity of Delhi to undertake unlawful activities. Those destined to be killed in fake encounters are not kept in police stations or at known facilities, they are lodged in these farm houses. They are detained for months and years there before they are killed at some "appropriate time".

These encounters usually take place in the evening or dead of night. A stolen vehicle and a gun is recovered. Those victims who are killed in such encounters are kidnapped in such a way that nobody knows their whereabouts. The sleuths also take care that no case is lodged against this kidnapping. If there is hue and cry, they will wait for things to cool down. The police of different states also exchange victims with each other. In every state, you have now special branches or cells or squads who directly take orders from the IB.

For example, Special Cell of Delhi Police will take two Kashmiris from the Special Operations Group (SoG) of Jammu and Kashmir Police and in exchange give them two persons from this side, who are killed in Kashmir branding them Pakistanis. Since they never get recognized and local people also show indifference, police stories look credible.

Since this game is played at a very high level, local police is a mute spectator. Most of the time they don't even know what is happening. Most of the time local police also treats it as a usual kidnapping case, when the families lodge complaint.

With all authority, I want to inform you that encounter orders come from higher authorities in the Home Ministry and all security agencies know an encounter is being managed on a particular day. A team which is designed to inspect the scene of encounter and report whether it was fake or not, prepares its report in advance, making this exercise also farce.

Have you ever noticed, that those killed in encounters carry all their details, their name, rank in the organization etc. in their pockets when they face encounter? Further, they die even without firing a bullet and even if they fire, it never hits the target. Our police needs to be appreciated that during past few years in almost 100 encounters, not a single personnel was ever injured. Compare it with the army's encounters with real terrorists in Kashmir. In almost every battle, one or two personnel get bullet wounds.

It speaks, either our army is not as trained as the Special Cell of Delhi Police, or the encounter is fake. If the Police insists on genuineness of these encounters, then I suggest, they be posted in Kashmir to replace army. People of this nation will also realize their bravery.

I will tell you how brave our Special Unit is. If they ever come to know that a miscreant is armed with a knife, they will never dare to go close to him. They will only nab him, when they are confident that the miscreant is unarmed. I have worked as their informer. They would make sure from us that the culprit is totally unarmed when they go to apprehend him.

Dear Sir, the Special Cell is a group of licensed marauders. They have been highly communalized. They are venomous against Muslims. They hardly bother that somebody's family gets ruined, they are only concerned with their own rewards. Let me say, these Special Cell personnel are just human bodies with an animal soul. And to speak of their torture techniques, it is beyond your imagination. Even more brutal than you see in films.

My only fault is that I refused to go along with them too long. They know, in the name of Islamic terrorism, you can book anyone, plant explosive, give name of some organization and make some hue and cry in the media. Rest with great distress, I am pained to say, our courts too fall in line. I was in their confinement for over two months. When my father lodged a complaint in local police station and the family of my co-accused Nawab S/o Qamar gave a look-out notice on TV, then they produced us claiming, "we nabbed them with explosives when they were returning after two month training". We challenged it in the High Court. High Court later directed the CBI to inquire, which has submitted its preliminary report. I don't think they will go too far to book their cousins in the IB and Special Cell. For past one-and-half year, we have been identifying the place, where we were kept for two months. But, they are deliberately ignoring to put it on record.

I appeal to the Prime Minister Dr. Manmohan Singh to step in and put a stop on such activities. These agencies are not securing the country, but making it extremely insecure. Those youth, who could contribute in nation building, are consigned to jails or encounters. If we book a young man with dreams to do something for a nation, in a fake case and make him a terrorist, it is foolish to believe that he remains loyal to you.

People who are jailed in such fake cases do think that if they ought to be punished heavily, then it was better for them to get arrested after really doing something. This is a dangerous trend. A rebellious thinking takes over. Even if they are released, no one is ready to own them.

Dear Prime Minister, it is high time to give a message to your security agencies. Fire can never douse fire. It needs water. Your security agencies are dousing fire with petrol.

I wish you to read the CBI report which has been submitted in the High Court, which clearly mentions names of the IB officers for whom I was working as an informer. And who also kidnapped me.

Here are names and number of officials for whom I was working:

- IB officer Khalid alias Majid 9810702004
- IB officer Aftab 9810702004
- ACP Sanjeev Yadav 9810058002
- Inspector Lalit Mohan, Hardev Bhushan 9811980604, 8711980601

- They had given me also a mobile phone with SIM 9873303646
- My mobile for talking to IB officers 9873131845

It is not difficult for any agency or the media to get details of calls from these numbers to dig out truth.

Yours only

Irshad Ali S/o Mohamamd Yunus,

Ward No 5 (High Risk) Cell No. 13, Jail No. 8,
Tihar, Delhi 110064.

Appendix III

A five-judge bench of the Andhra Pradesh High Court, having deliberated on a clutch of writ petitions filed between 1999 and 2008, under article 226 of the Constitution of India, pertaining to encounter killings in the State pronounced its judgement on 6 February 2009. This bench framed four issues for consideration (see "Death by Encounter" for details on the four questions). The bench's judgement was a voluminous 50,000-word long, profound reading of substantive law, a meditation on Article 21 and a masterly survey of case law. Reproduced here is a section from the Court's observations in response to Issue number 1, namely, "Where a police officer causes the death of a person, acting or purporting to act in discharge of official duties or in self-defence as the case may be, is there commission of a cognizable offence (including in an appropriate case the offence of culpable homicide)".

* * *

The Andhra Pradesh Police Officers' Association would urge that Section 154 (1) Cr.P.C., on text and principle accommodates a discretion in the recording officer, to consider whether a complaint conveying information as to the commission of a cognizable offence together with the factual narrative indicating a claim to one or more of the general exceptions (in Chapter-IV IPC) requires to be registered as FIR. In view of the provisions of Section 6 IPC the offences enumerated in the Code must be read subject to the provisions of Chapter-IV IPC and therefore contends Sri Uday Lalit (the learned senior counsel, for the 10th respondent[1]), the recording officer acts within his inherent discretion under Section 154 (1) Cr.P.C. in declining to record the information and registering the FIR when the complaint conveys information that facially indicates commission of a cognizable offence but taken together with the general exceptions in Chapter-IV IPC (since the information also claims the benefit of one or more of these exceptions), the information does not convey facts disclosing commission of a cognizable offence and hence does not warrant registering the FIR. It is further contended that to interpret the provisions in Section 154 (1) Cr.P.C. otherwise would lead to disastrous consequences. The elaboration in this regard is that wherever a complaint is made, for instance as to deprivation of life or liberty by judicial authority or pursuant to a judgment or order of a Court; by a child under seven (7) years of age or by a child above seven (7) and under twelve (12) but of immature understanding; by a person of unsound mind; or by a medical authority, it would be obligatory for the recording officer to register a FIR and set the investigatorial process into motion. Such a result would destabilize equilibrium and would be productive of immense and avoidable public mischief, is the contention.

In our considered view these apprehensions are misplaced. Sections 77 and 78 IPC carve out a general exception from culpability in favour of judicial authority or acts done pursuant to a judgment or an order of a Court. Where the information conveyed is that the conduct complained of is by a judicial authority or pursuant to a judgment or an order of the Court, the information is inherently not as to the commission of any offence (in view of Sec. 6 r/w Sec. 77 & 78 IPC); further convictions and sentences are by the Court, the officer performing the functions of office. Where however the information is to the effect that a person masquerading as judge or not acting in such capacity had committed a cognizable offence, then and in such circum-

---

1 M/s Andhra Pradesh Police Officers Association represented by its General Secretary Mr. KV Ram Narasimha Reddy, office at Lakdikapool, Hyderabad.

stance the recording officer must record the information and register the same as a First Information Report. We perceive no serious or grave public mischief ensuing as a consequence of interpreting Section 154 (1) Cr.P.C. on its normal textual terms.

It requires to be noticed that Article 261 of the Constitution enjoins that Full faith and credit shall be given throughout the territory of India to public acts, records and judicial proceedings of the Union and of every State. The appointment of a judge is a public act and the particulars and designation of appointment as a judge are matters of public record. Even if a mischievous complaint is made that a named individual masquerading as a judge had passed an order; whether the named individual is a judge is an easily discoverable public act and a matter of public record. Even the provisions of Section 81 of the Evidence Act enjoin that a Court shall presume the genuineness of any official gazette or government gazette. Judicial appointments of every hue and hierarchy through out the territory of India are gazetted appointments.

For reasons alike, as discussed in the preceding paragraphs, complaints against persons entitled to incompetence defenses such as infants (Sections 82 and 83 IPC) or against medical authority (Sections 88, 89 and 92 IPC) may either require to be recorded and registered as FIR or not, depending upon the idiosyncratic facts, context and circumstances of the information. In any event, the failure to record the information or register the FIR wherever warranted by law, is productive of far greater public mischief than the inconvenience occasioned by recording and registering the FIR.

It must also be recognized that the exceptions in favour of judicial authority or the immunity vouchsafed to acts done pursuant to an order or judgment of a Court comprise public policy class of defenses. The language of Sections 77 and 78 IPC shows that the exculpation is absolute and not hedged in by limitations as in the case of private/self-defense justifications. As we have earlier herein considered on analyses of the textual, juridical and precendential exposition of defense justifications, private defense is a right available as only a preventive and not a retributive measure and proportionality of the defensive force employed to an initial aggression, is an integral component that defines the contours of justifiable claims to a defensive force justification. The general exceptions enumerated in favour of judicial authority or in respect of acts done pursuant to a judgment or order of the Court are thus qualitatively dissimilar and provide an absolute exculpation. We perceive no substance in this contention except sophistry.

Empirical analysis, textual and curial authority with respect to self defense justifications considered supra indicates that the need of self-preservation is rooted in the doctrine of necessity. It is the rule of necessity to which a party may have a recourse under certain situations to prevent greater personal injury or injury to others which he may apprehend. Self-preservation is more an instinctive than a cognitive condition of a majority of the living species and in particular human beings. This instinct is recognized a lawful defense in the laws of civilized Nations and finds legislative expression in Sections 96 to 106 IPC. These statutory provisions per se and as expounded in decisions are clearly to the effect that the Exceptions are hedged in and circumscribed by conditions and limitations including the imminence and gravity (standard) of the threat and conditions as to the requirement of proportionality of the response/ defense.

The basic elements of self-defense by employment of deadly/lethal force include (1) the perpetrator must have reasonable grounds to believe that he was in imminent danger of death or serious body harm; heated words, vague threats or the possibility of future harm does not suffice; the harm must be serious and imminent; (2) the perpetrator actually believed that he or any other person was in such imminent danger; establishing this subjective belief may normally require the perpetrator to make a statement or testify as the case may be; (3) the danger was such that the perpetrator could only save himself by employment of deadly force; (4) the perpetrator had employed no more force than was necessary in all the circumstances of the case; and (5) the perpetrator was not the initial aggressor.

Self-defense justification is normally an all or nothing strategy. In order to establish it, the perpetrator has to admit being at the scene of offence with a weapon, which he used intentionally to harm the aggressor. He has to admit that he injured/killed the aggressor. The facts gathered must establish and in a given situation the perpetrator may have to establish that a reasonable person in his place would have acted similarly. Self-defense justifications normally imply a rational response to a very dangerous situation, and normally eschew claims of mental illness, insanity, defenses based on intoxication or drug use, or other defenses enumerated as General exceptions to criminality.

Conclusion on Issue No.1:

On a careful consideration of the relevant statutory provisions; the binding and persuasive precedents; the normative architecture of private defense justifications generally and in the context of the provisions of the IPC; and the constitutional values that inform and structure our governance processes, we hold that the information conveyed to the officer in charge of a Police Station intimating the death of any person as a consequence of firing by law enforcement officials of the State (notwithstanding a claim as to the death occurring while exercising the right of private defence) must invariably and without exception be registered as FIR u/Sec. 154(1) Cr.P.C.; and investigation u/ Sections 156/157 must follow.

Sri Kannabiran, the learned senior counsel (for the 9th respondent in W.P.No. 15419 of 2006[2]) cited the Privy Council decision in Palmer v. The Queen and the House of Lords' decision in R. v. Clegg to support the contention that if the plea of self-defense fails in a case resulting in death in an encounter between civilians and police, the conviction for murder under Section 302 IPC must necessarily follow. We refrain from pronouncing on this aspect of the matter as this aspect does not fall for consideration before this Bench per se or as integral to any of the issues formulated for our consideration.

The question whether on the failure of a plea of self-defense, in cases of death resulting from a police encounter, the accused police officer(s) must invariably be convicted for murder or may be convicted for culpable homicide not amounting to murder, is an aspect that is more appropriately determined by the appropriate Court of Session when trying the charge.

---

2 Peoples Union for Civil Liberties.

Appendix IV

Reproduced here is an extract from the judgement in *State vs. Saqib Rehman @Masood and Others* (SC No. 24/10) pronounced in the Court of Additional Sessions Judge Virender Bhat. For details of the case, see the chapter "Crime and Punishment" in Section II. The Court acquitted the accused and directed the registering of FIR against the police officers, holding them culpable for framing innocents in a terror case.

In re. : Defence of the accused

134. Since the case put forward by the prosecution against these accused has fallen flat and it has been established that the encounter so projected by the police was an absolutely fake and stage managed, the defence put forward by the accused that they are innocent and have been framed up falsely in this case gains credence. Even otherwise, it has been proved on record by DW1 Gulam Moinuddin Dar (one of the accused) that he has been engaged in anti militancy operations in J&K and has got more than 300 militants surrendered in Kashmir valley. The other accused Bashir Ahmed Shah was his friend and paid the price for the same. The third accused Saqib-ur-Rehman also used to give valuable inputs to J&K police about various anti social elements. The other accused were ordinary citizens and no criminal or terrorism related background has been proved in their case.

In re : Conclusion

135. Viewed from any angle, the encounter alleged to have been taken place on the night intervening between 01.7.05 and 02.7.05, did not take place at all and an absolutely fake encounter has been projected. The story of the encounter was carefully scripted in the office of Special Staff, Delhi Police, Dhaula Kuan, by its main author SI Ravinder Tyagi with the assistance of SI Nirakar, SI Charan Singh and SI Mahender Singh. All these four police officers have acted in advancement of their self interests in total disregard to the demands of their solemn duty. These four police officers whose duty was to protect and safeguard the citizens, have turned persecutors and tormentors.

136. The aim of the investigating agency is to collect evidence and not to create it. Its aim should be to discover the truth. It is not only unethical but also illegal for an investigating agency to resort to concoction, paddling, fabrication of evidence – all serious offences under the law - even to bring a known criminal to justice. Its relevance in India is much felt as there are no defence investigators as there are in various western countries. Hence the machinery of criminal law is often used here as a handy weapon to wreak vengeance on the enemy.

137. Fabrication of false encounter is not justified in any social set-up where the rule of law prevails even if the person, so apprehended, is really a terrorist or otherwise, harmful to the society. In India, a section of some over-zealous, overambitious and scrupulous police officers is seen, who seem to think that if a person is really harmful to the society, there is no problem in creating some evidence or supplying the missing link in the evidence to secure his conviction. If fabrication of false evidence were to be justified because of a laudable motive, the worst criminal on earth would justify the worst crime on the ground of good motive.

138. In the present case, the prosecution has failed to produce any evidence to show that the accused persons are in fact, terrorists having links with the ISI Agency of Pakistan. No investigation has been conducted in this regard by the Delhi Police. It has failed to trace out the source of the arms/ammunition allegedly recovered from and at the instance of the accused as also that of the fake currency notes. No investigation has been

carried out in Gurgaon from where the accused allegedly came to Delhi alongwith arms/ammunition. The secret information received by SI Ravinder Tyagi has turned out to be absolutely concocted. So, where was the justification for the raid and encounter.

139. See the plight of these seven accused, out of whom five have been languishing in jail for about five and a half years now for no fault of theirs. They are totally innocent and have been framed in this case by the aforesaid four police officers in order to achieve their personal gains and/or to settle petty personal scores, be that at the behest of one Major Sharma, whose attempts to persuade accused Gulam Moinuddin Dar to work for him in getting the militants surrendered in Kashmir were spurned by him (Gulam Moinuddin Dar) or to earn undue honours or awards for themselves. In today's aspirational world of glitter, fine dining and mall culture, only money and material matters. The values such as service to the nation, integrity and honesty are becoming rare.

140. All the accused are liable to be acquitted and are hereby acquitted honourably. I cannot resist reading out a prayer to these accused which a Canadian Lady Judge read out to a prisoner, whom she had to free after spending 26 years in prison. The prayer is :

Dear friends,
May the road rise to meet you,
May the wind be always at your back,
May the Sun shine warm on your face,
May the rain fall softly upon you,
May God hold you in the palm of his hand, now and forever.

141. I go again back to the stage managing of the fake encounter by the four police officials namely SI Ravinder Tyagi, SI Nirakar, SI Charan Singh and SI Mahender Singh, as it is difficult to take it out of mind. These four police officers have brought utter shame and disrepute to the whole Delhi Police Force. In my opinion, there cannot be any more serious or grave crime than a police officer framing an innocent citizen in a false criminal case. Such tendency in the police officers should not be viewed or dealt with lightly but needs to be curbed with a

stern hand. It is because of such brazen acts of a few policemen that the general public is losing faith in the whole police system. Such black sheep, who are out to defame and bring into disrepute the whole police force, need to be identified from the whole flock and taken to task.

142. I, therefore, direct the Commissioner of Police, Delhi, to initiate appropriate inquiry against the four police officers SI Ravinder Tyagi, SI Nirakar, SI Charan Singh and SI Mahender Singh (who by now may have been promoted to the post Inspector) for the misuse and abuse of their powers as a police officer, as detailed herein-above. The inquiry shall be completed within three months from today, and report be submitted to this Court on the next date of hearing.

143. The SHO, Police Station Kapasahera is also directed to register FIR against the aforesaid four police officers U/s.167 IPC and forward the same to the Addl. Commissioner of Police (South/West) who shall conduct investigation which shall be completed within three months from today and a report be submitted to this Court on the next date of hearing. A copy of the FIR shall be sent to this Court within one month from today.

144. A copy of this judgment be sent to the concerned Magistrate dealing with the cases of police station Kapasahera with directions to treat the same as a complaint against SI Ravinder Tyagi, SI Nirakar, SI Charan Singh and SI Mahender Singh of Delhi Police for offences punishable U/s.166, 193 and 195 IPC and to proceed with the same as per law.

145. Before concluding, I would like to remind the whole Delhi Police force about the disconcerting note sounded by Abraham Lincolon:

If you once forfeit the confidence of our fellow citizens, you can never regain their respect and esteem. It is true that you can fool all the people some of the time and some of the people all the time, but you cannot fool all the people all the time.

...

Announced in open Court on 02.2.2011.
(VIRENDER BHAT) A.S.J.: Dwarka Courts
New Delhi.

Index

www.ingramcontent.com/pod-product-compliance
Lightning Source LLC
Chambersburg PA
CBHW062135160726
48282CB00027B/837
* 9 7 8 9 3 8 3 9 6 8 0 0 8 *